Christmas in Poland

Cover photo: *People of all ages come to admire the crèches entered in the annual competition held in Kraków's Rynek Główny, one of the largest town squares in Europe.*

Christmas in Poland

**Christmas Around the World
From World Book**

World Book, Inc.
a Scott Fetzer company
Chicago

Christmas in Poland was prepared by the Editorial and Art Departments of World Book, Inc.

Printed in the United States of America.

ISBN 0-7166-0889-8
Library of Congress Catalog Card No. 89-50196
a/hi

The publisher wishes to thank the many individuals who took part in developing this publication. Special thanks go to Zofia Sadlińska-Kaspar and Ellen Wierzewski of the Copernicus Foundation of Chicago.

Special appreciation also goes to Villeroy & Bock Tableware, Ltd. for their contribution to the recipe cards.

Contents

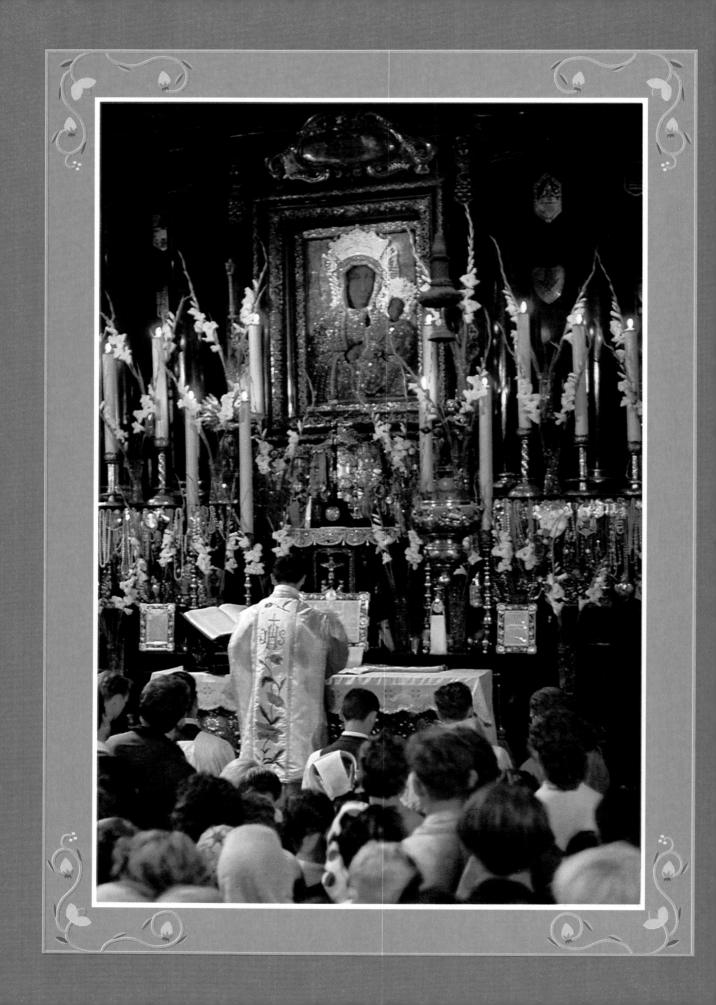

A National Tradition

In Poland, Christmas has been the holiest and most festive occasion of the year for many centuries. Since the conversion of the Polish people to Christianity in 966 under Duke Mieszko I, Christmas has been gradually adorned with religious ceremonies and rich folk traditions. In much the same manner, the sacred picture of Our Lady at the national shrine in Częstochowa has been adorned with jewels and precious metals. Polish Christmas traditions shine through the centuries with a richness of beauty, variety, religious feeling, and playful folklore.

To appreciate the loyalty and spirit Poles have for these Christmas traditions it is important to understand Poland's history during much of the past 200 years. Before 1772, Poland ruled a vast empire covering much of eastern Europe. However, by 1795, Poland no longer existed as a separate country. The land, and its people, were divided among three neighboring countries: Russia, Prussia, and Austria. After years of struggle, Poland became an independent republic once again in 1918. Independence was short-lived, however. In 1939, at the beginning of World War II, Poland was once again divided—this time invaded by the Union of Soviet Socialist Republics (U.S.S.R.) and Germany.

Our Lady of Częstochowa, also known as the "Black Madonna," is a Gothic painting very sacred to the people of Poland. Częstochowa is a town which lies on the Warta River in south-central Poland. The Black Madonna is inside a monastery's baroque church atop a small hill known as Jasna Góra.

Agreements made at the end of the war shifted Poland's borders. In 1945, a new, smaller Poland was formed. Today those same borders exist. Most of Poland's 120,728 square miles (312,683 square kilometers) consist of vast plains and gently rolling hills. This is about the same size as New Mexico in the United States. A little over half of Poland's northern boundary is formed by the coastline of the Baltic Sea. On the south, rugged mountains form part of its boundary with Czechoslovakia. To the west, the Oder and Neisse rivers form the border with East Germany. On the east, there are virtually no natural boundaries with the Soviet Union. It is this lack of natural boundaries that has made Poland prey to other countries.

Poles are very much aware of their history and how it has shaped their national heritage.

*Przed twe ołtarze zanosim
    błaganie.
Ojczyznę wolnaz racz nam
    wrócić Panie.*
Before your altar, Lord, we
    carry our petition.
Grant us once again our free
    homeland.

Mountains in the Podhale region of Poland make up part of Poland's border to the south.

Religious beliefs, including Christmas traditions, held the Polish people together through the many years of war and separation. Celebrating old Polish traditions—although in the privacy of their homes—was the closest Poles could come to being with distant loved ones. Although they could not be together physically as a country, they could be together spiritually. These traditions allowed parents to pass on the Polish culture to their children, thus keeping that culture alive into future generations. These traditions have united with Christian creed and custom to weave a faith that has kept Poland Polish and Catholic through the centuries.

Christmas traditions have formed a bond between Poland's past and its present. Over a thousand years of Polish

Much of Poland is covered by flat plains. These snow-covered plains are in southern Poland.

Christmases have built one of the sturdy pillars upon which its culture stands proudly. Over a thousand years of Polish Christmases go into each *opłatek* (Christmas wafer), each *kolęda*, or Christmas carol, that is sung, each prayer that is whispered to the Christ child.

When a garland is hung about the *choinka*, or Christmas tree, it may be remembered that straw garlands shaped like chains were used in the nineteenth century. Those garlands symbolized the chains that foreign domination had placed around Poland. When Christmas carols are sung, perhaps they are sung extra loud. This might be an effort to make up for all those years when public singing in the Polish language was forbidden; even the use of the language in schools and public buildings was outlawed. When an extra place setting at the *Wigilia*, or Christmas Eve, table is set and an empty chair is put in place, perhaps it will be done for "an unexpected guest" or in memory of a friend or relative who is not able to be home for Wigilia.

The entire cycle of Polish holidays that surrounds Christmas begins with Advent (four weeks before Christmas) and usually continues through January 6, the Feast of the Three Kings, with some Poles celebrating the season through February 2, the Feast of the Purification of Our Lady. The cycle includes

a number of feast days in honor of special saints. Each of these days has its own religious observances, folk customs (not always observed), and sometimes even special meals.

Many Polish Christmas traditions are virtually unchanged from their inception centuries ago. Saint Nicholas still brings small gifts for children as he always has. The opłatek is broken and shared on Wigilia,

A Christmas tree made of lights decorates a street in the city of Warsaw.

Christmas Eve, as so often before. But there are other traditions that have been adapted to changing times. *Pająki*, uniquely decorated mobiles hung from the ceiling, have given way to *podlaźniki*, tops of evergreen trees hung upside down from the ceiling and decorated. These, in turn, have made way for the modern choinka, or Christmas tree, usually a small evergreen tree decorated with both homemade and store-bought decorations.

Two calamitious world wars in the 1900's have brought many changes to Poland. Many customs and traditions have disappeared from everyday life. However, Christmas as a national tradition has retained its uniquely Polish character. Christmas is still celebrated today in recognizably the same way as in centuries past.

A Family Tradition

Christmas has always been a family celebration in Poland. Not only does the family feast and pray together on the various days of this holiday season, but it also works together to prepare for the twelve days of Christmas, known as *Gody*.

The Christmas tree is set up and decorated by everyone in the household. If the decorations are to be homemade, then the whole family helps in making them. In addition, children who have made decorations at school bring them home for the whole family to enjoy. Everyone also contributes to decorating the home. Other projects are done together as much as possible. Christmas greeting cards have to be sent. Cooking and baking must be done. A special honey spice cake known as *piernik* should be made two or three weeks before Wigilia. The opłatek also has to be obtained well in advance of Christmas.

Before Christmas trees made their appearance in Poland, homes were decorated with handmade mobiles suspended from the ceiling. Although called *pajaki*, meaning *spiders*, these mobiles rather more resembled spider webs, very intricate in their ornament and design. The mobile originally began as a wreath made with the best grains grown the previous summer. Festooned with nuts, apples, and delicate spherical sculptures made of unleavened wafers, these wreaths were sometimes hung directly over the dining table where the Wigilia supper was to be held.

Traveling to town in the snowy weather of winter is no problem when you get a free ride. This family is going shopping together in preparation for the Christmas season.

A couple tries to choose a choinka, or *Christmas tree, off a lot in Warsaw.* (top) *The modern Christmas tree is a fairly new tradition in Poland. Carrying home the chosen tree is no problem for this gentleman.* (bottom) *But will there be enough decorations to cover it?*

Eventually, the wreaths were expanded upon and could end up to be quite large. Paper cutouts in the shapes of stars, flowers, or crosses could be added. Colored tissue paper could be used for the cutouts, which would then be mounted on pieces of straw before being attached to the mobile. Straw was used to make chains to hang around them. Feathers were also a popular addition. Everything blended together to form a mobile of delicate beauty and Polish tradition.

The modern Christmas tree was introduced in Poland during the nineteenth century. By the second half of that century, urban Poles began putting up Christmas trees. In the countryside, where most Poles lived at the time, the "new innovation" was not readily accepted. Most Poles preferred their traditional mobile. In southern Poland, however, the practice of suspending the tops of fir trees upside down from the ceiling began. These trees, called podlaźniki, were decorated with apples, nuts, and candy. Eventually, small dolls and toy soldiers were often added.

Throughout the twentieth century, the Christmas tree gained in popularity, as the mobiles and upside-down tops of trees declined in popularity. Since the 1920's, the Christmas tree has become the most visible symbol of Christmas in the Polish home. Seldom if ever do Polish families cut down their own tree in the forest anymore. Today, most buy their tree in stores. Traditional Polish tree decorations include home-made garlands made of tissue paper and cut straw; paper cut-outs in the shapes of angels, candles, and stars; apples, nuts, candy, and little cakes. Increasingly more popular in Poland are store-bought decorations. These include strings of electric lights, Christmas ornaments, cotton, and tinsel. Artificial trees have also made their appearance in Polish homes, much to the chagrin of many a purist.

Other popular tree decorations include strings of peas, beans, and corn. Blown eggs have been used for a long time as well. Eggs, being symbols of the miracle of birth, are very appropriate to the holidays. After the eggshells are drained, they can be turned into a variety of fanciful ornaments: angels, small pitchers, flower-

pots, doves (symbolizing peace), or roosters (symbolizing health and fertility). The shells can also be painted with the face of an angel or a clown or someone from Poland's long and colorful history.

Despite the increasing use of electric lights on Christmas trees, many families still prefer to use candles. Candles with their burning flames have much meaning and symbolism in Polish culture. They are lit during baptismal and matrimonial ceremonies, at First Holy Communion ceremonies, and on birthdays. It is thus very appropriate to also light candles for the birthday of the Christ child.

Underneath the tree, a *szopka*, or Christmas crèche scene, is usually placed, along with the gifts on Christmas Eve. The tree can be set up and trimmed anytime during Advent, although traditionally it is not done until the after-noon of Wigilia. In some households, the tree then stands until January 6, the Feast of the Three Kings. In others, however, the tree stands until February 2, the Feast of the Purification of Our Lady—the official ending of the Christmas season in Poland.

The practice of sending Christmas cards is a fairly recent holiday tradition. The

A woman carefully examines the decorations for sale at a market in Warsaw. Store-bought Christmas tree decorations are becoming increasingly popular in Poland.

Decorating the home for the Christmas season is a family affair. Dressed in traditional Polish costume, this family sings kolędy, *or Christmas carols, while decorating the tree.*

Englishman John Calcott Horsley is usually credited with creating the first Christmas card around the middle of the nineteenth century. Polish Christmas cards are very beautiful, often combining folk motifs with various religious symbols of Christmas. Poles usually write in their own holiday greeting before signing the cards. They also often include a piece of opłatek in cards sent to friends and relatives.

Piernik, or honey spice cake, is often baked in the early days of December. It is baked this early because its flavor improves with aging. In Poland today, there are several bakeries that make this honey spice cake in quantity. One is in Toruń, a city on the Wisła (Vistula) River northwest of Warsaw. Nuns of the Order of St. Catherine were once so famous for their delicious pierniki that the little cakes became known as *Katarzynki*, or little Catherines. Toruń is also famous as the birthplace of the Polish astronomer Nicolaus Copernicus. The piernik bakery there is named after him, the Kopernik. Another bakery famous for its honey spice cake is the Wawel in Kraków, the beautiful former capital of Poland situated on the banks of the Wisła (Vistula) in southern Poland. Wawel Castle is a former royal castle in Kraków. The Wawel bakery, which is named after the castle, also makes many delicious confections, candies, chocolates, and other cakes besides pierniki. Polish pierniki are very famous all over the world, and are often exported.

Piernik may be baked in various shapes. In former

centuries, these might be knights, various animals, or the Polish kings of yesteryear. Today, most have more traditional Christmas shapes: Saint Nicholas, a reindeer, a star, or a heart. Some are frosted and some are plain. And they are always appropriate as Christmas tree ornaments.

Schoolchildren in Lublin, a town in southeastern Poland, make Christmas decorations for their school and homes. (left) Polish children send Christmas cards to friends and relatives. (below)

Advent:
The Saints Rejoice

The word *advent* comes from the Latin word *adventus*, meaning *arrival* or *coming*. Advent is a time of religious preparation for the arrival of the Christ child. Long ago in Poland, Advent lasted for a period of forty days, the same length of time as Lent, which is the period between Ash Wednesday and Easter Sunday, when Christians show sorrow for sins and seek forgiveness. At that time, Advent started on the Feast of Saint Martin, November 11. Today, Advent does not begin until the fourth Sunday before Christmas. Nevertheless, several customs associated with St. Martin's Day are still observed in Poland. And many Poles celebrate the day with the traditional roast goose dinner.

Saint Martin is a patron saint of Poznań, a city lying on the Warta River in west-central Poland. In the A.D. 900's, Poznań became the seat of the first Catholic bishopric in Poland. Together with Gniezno, Poland's first capital about 30 miles (48 kilometers) to the east of Poznań, this region became the nucleus of the emerging Polish state. Equally proud of their patron saint as they are of their heritage, the people of Poznań remember him on his day by special observances in St. Martin's Church. There is also a singular type of bread roll baked on this day. In the shape of a crescent moon, it is known as *drożdżowy rogal świętomarciński,* or St. Martin's crescent roll.

Saint Nicholas leaves a home after a visit with the children. According to tradition, he brings with him sweets and toys for the "good" and coal for the "bad." St. Nicholas Day (December 6) is one of the more popular saint's days during Advent in Poland, especially for children.

A detail of a painting of Saint Andrew. He was the first of the twelve apostles of Jesus Christ. St. Andrew's Day (November 30) is primarily celebrated by the young in Poland.

of strict fast and abstinence. This meant that meals were smaller and often without meat. The roast goose dinner was thus the last full meal before the big feast on Christmas Eve.

The meal can even involve a bit of fortunetelling. The bones of the goose could be read to foretell how the winter would be.

Patrz na piersi, patrz na kości, jaka zima nam zagości.
Gdy się woda ścina i pierś gęsi biała,
będzie zima stała.
Look at the breast, look at the bones,
what kind of a guest winter will be.
If the water congeals and the breast is white,
winter will be long and hard.

St. Martin's Day is also considered unofficially to be the first day of winter. There are many proverbs linking the saint to the coming of winter. One of the most popular is *Święty Marcin na białym koniu jedzie* (Saint Martin is riding on a white horse), which would be a sign that winter is close at hand or already here.

According to tradition, the big evening dinner on St. Martin's Day includes roast goose. This practice started in the days when Advent was forty days long and a season

When the first day of Advent was pushed up to the fourth Sunday before Christmas, the preseasonal festivities shifted to the last several days of November, centering around the feast days of Saint Catherine (November 25) and Saint Andrew (November 30). Although there are no special meals or religious ceremonies at this time, young Poles may still fill the days with merrymaking and dancing, and more fortunetelling. These activities began at a time when dancing would have been strictly

On St. Catherine's Day (November 25) a young man may place a cherry tree twig in water or wet soil. If the twig produces a blossom by Christmas, the young man can look forward to becoming married in the coming year.

forbidden during Advent. Although such a prohibition no longer exists, the tradition of throwing a party on St. Andrew's Day still persists in many parts of Poland.

Saint Catherine is regarded in Poland as the patron saint of young men. The eve of St. Catherine's Day (November 24) was often the scene of all-male parties called *kawalerskie wieczory*, usually held in taverns. Later that night, if a young man wanted to discover whom he would marry, he would write out the names of all the eligible young women in whom he might be interested. Each name was written on a separate small piece of paper. The papers were then placed under his pillow. When he awoke at dawn, he would reach under his pillow and pull out one of the pieces of paper. He would then know who was to be his future wife.

Alternatively, if the young man only wanted to know whether he would soon marry, and not whom he would marry, he could simply break a twig off a cherry tree. He would then plant it carefully in wet soil or place it in a vase. In either case, he tended it until Christmas. If the twig blossomed, he could expect to be married within the coming year. If not, he would have to wait another year before finding himself a wife.

The customs of St. Catherine's Day are less observed today in Poland than are the customs of St. Andrew's Day. According to tradition, Saint Andrew preached the Gospel in eastern Europe.

One of the more popular activities on St. Andrew's Day (November 30) involves wax. The shape of the wax gives clues as to whom a girl will marry.

One of the sayings that is often recited around St. Andrew's Day and St. Catherine's Day is *Święty Jędrzej adwent przytwierdzi.* (Saint Andrew confirms the Advent.) On these days it was believed that the merrymaking and dancing start with Saint Catherine and end with Saint Andrew. *Katarzyna rada podskakuje; Święty Andrzej zakazuje.* (Catherine jumps with joy; St. Andrew forbids such levity.)

Because weddings were once not allowed during Advent, a series of fortune-telling traditions evolved. By means of these traditions, a young Polish woman could read the future and find out if and when she would marry, and even whom she would marry. Although similar to the auguries for young men on St. Catherine's Eve, these fortune-telling traditions for young women on St. Andrew's Day

were more varied and complex.

The most popular was, and still is, the pouring of wax. First of all, wax is melted in a saucepan. While the wax is melting, a bowl of cold water is prepared. The first girl who wishes to see her matrimonial future then pours a bit of the melted wax into the cold water. She waits a few moments for it to harden, and then removes the piece of formed wax from the bowl. She now holds it near a candle flame (but not too close) or near a lamp in such a way as to cast its shadow on the wall. The shape of the shadow is then interpreted. The young girl looks hard to see the form of a bridal wreath, which would be a sign of impending marriage. Or perhaps she espies the shape of

a bee or a book. Would she marry a beekeeper or a writer? She may also look for the form of a computer, maybe even a spaceship, because these days it is not impossible that she may marry a computer analyst or an astronaut. She may even look harder and see a slender human form or a considerably larger one. Would her husband be thin or fat? Perhaps she sees nothing at all. She will have to try again, after all the other girls have had their chance.

Another way of telling a young woman's marital future also involves a bowl of water. Each girl writes the name of her boyfriend on a small piece of paper. The papers are then attached to the inside rim of a bowl of water. A small candle

Young girls spend much of St. Andrew's Day (November 30) in fortunetelling activities. Whose paper will burn first? A burnt paper means a marriage proposal in the coming year!

Lining up slippers heel-to-toe predicts someone's matrimonial future. The owner of the first shoe to cross the threshold can look forward to being the first to wed.

traditions are associated with St. Andrew's Day. As the boys do on St. Catherine's Day, the girls can also place slips of paper containing names of eligible boys under their pillows. Or they can carefully tend their own cherry tree twigs, hoping for a blossom by Christmas. Dreams are also especially significant on the eve of St. Catherine's Day. Dreaming of men can mean a speedy end to a young woman's maidenhood. Dreaming of a cradle could obviously mean the birth of a baby, or, by extension, an impending marriage. It would not be good to dream of a dog, as this might signify the dreamer will remain unmarried into old age.

One more popular fortune-telling game has the girls lining up their slippers from the wall opposite the house (or apartment) entrance to the threshold of that entrance. The slippers are placed in a straight line heel-to-toe. If there are not enough slippers to reach the threshold, the one set down first is brought up to the front, then the second, and so on. This is repeated until a slipper crosses the threshold. Its owner will then become the first to be married.

Still another custom is similar to the shell game, involving rather three cooking pots, saucepans, or soup bowls. Under one is placed a kerchief (sometimes a ring or a man's

is placed inside a walnut shell, which is then set afloat inside the bowl. The girls start blowing at the walnut shell, each trying to get the candle to burn the piece of paper with her boyfriend's name on it. A burned piece of paper means a marriage proposal from the boy sometime in the coming year.

Many other fortunetelling

hat); under another, a rosary (sometimes a piece of bread); and under the third, a ribbon. A girl is then blindfolded and spins around three times, while the pots or bowls are arranged. While still blindfolded, she chooses one of the three pots or bowls. If she chooses the kerchief, she will soon be wed. If the rosary, she will become a nun or remain unmarried all her life. If the ribbon, she will stay single for another year.

Other feast days during Advent include those of Saint Barbara (December 4), Saint Nicholas (December 6), Saint Lucy (December 13), and Saint Thomas (December 21).

Saint Barbara is a patron saint of miners and sailors. As such, there may be special commemorations in her honor in the churches of Silesia, a region in the uplands of southern Poland. One of the world's largest coal fields lies around Katowice, a major city of Silesia. Saint Barbara may also be specially commemorated in churches along Poland's over 300 miles (480 kilometers) of coastline, which borders the Baltic Sea in the north. According to old custom, the weather on December 4 foreshadows the weather at Christmas. *Święta Barbara po lodzie, Boże Narodzenie po wodzie.* (If ice on St. Barbara's, then rain on Christmas.)

By far, the most dearly beloved saint during Advent is

The Christmas season in Poland is filled with predictions about the weather. This snowy day may be foreshadowing the weather of Christmas.

Saint Nicholas, whose special day is December 6. His feast day is a "children's holiday" in Poland. Saint Nicholas was a bishop of Myra in Asia Minor (present-day Turkey) during the A.D. 300's. He was renowned for his piety and his generosity and kindness to children, with orphans occupying a special place in his heart.

Saint Nicholas, dressed in the more traditional costume, entertains school-children in Kraków. He wants to know if the children have been "good" or "bad" in the past year.

An old Polish children's song runs like this:

Saint Nicholas went into town
And bought himself some
  cakes.
Saint Nicholas, don't sit by the
  roadside!
People coming from the town
  will take your money,
Will take your money,
Will take your ducats. (a type
  of old coin)
What will you have then to
  give the poor and the needy
And the little children?
He gave and he gave
Until everything was gone.
He went to heaven, where he
  was given bread
And butter and Polish sausage,
Because these are days of
  plenty.

In Poland, the custom of giving gifts to children began in the first half of the eighteenth century. At that time, the gifts included honey spice cakes, a type of pretzel known as *obwarzanki*, holy cards, toys, and warm clothing. In memory of Saint Nicholas' generosity, parents would place gifts in the rooms of their sleeping children sometime during the night between the eve and the day of the saint's feast (December 5-6). The gifts were also intended to be a spur to greater piety, in memory of Saint Nicholas' renowned piety. When the children discovered the gifts on the following morning, the

Children of the village of Suchy Bor, near Warsaw, visit with Saint Nicholas. This young boy has assured Saint Nicholas that he has been well behaved in the past year. His reward: plenty of treats!

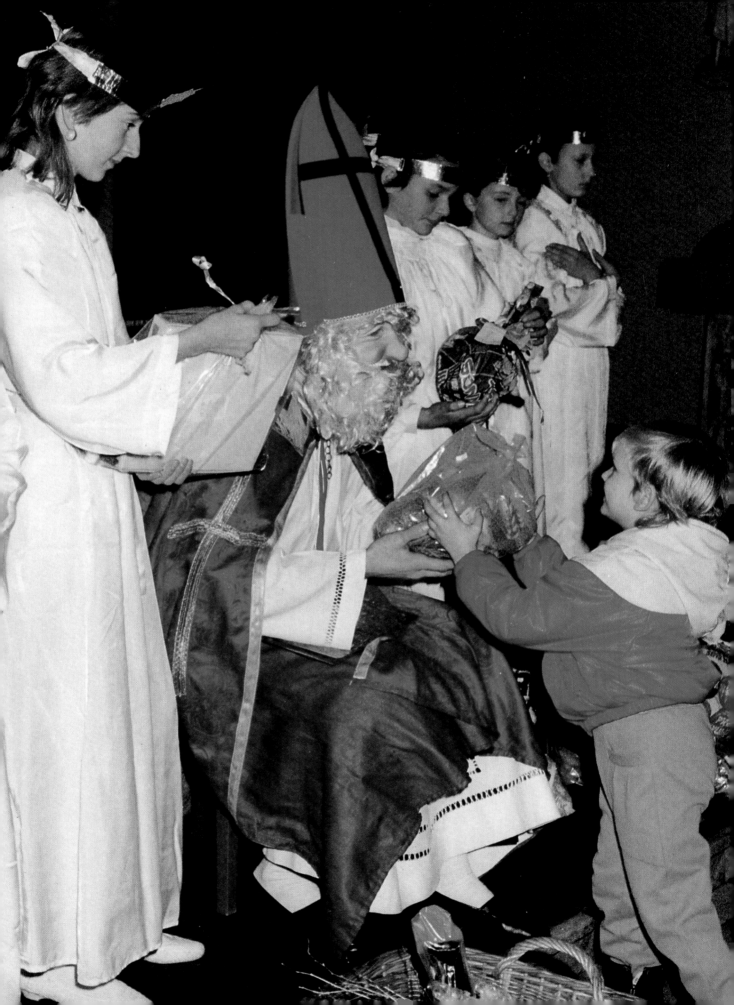

Saint Nicholas visits a group of excited schoolchildren. He is dressed in the more modern costume of Santa Claus. Saint Nicholas and Santa Claus are the same person to children of Poland.

sleigh. He would have long, white hair and a flowing white beard. He would wear a long, white robe, sometimes trimmed in fur, have on a tall hat, like a bishop's miter, and carry a shepherd's staff. Saint Nicholas might first ask a child to recite the "Lord's Prayer." Satisfied as to the child's piety, he would then ask whether he or she had been a good little boy or girl. If good, the gift could be a cake or pastry, candy or pudding, holy cards, or big red apples. If bad, the child might receive a lump of coal. However, most children would know better than to misbehave around St. Nicholas' Day. There would be very few naughty children then!

This custom has survived to the present day throughout most of Poland. A person dressed as Saint Nicholas may ride the streets of Polish villages. In large towns and cities, he might visit a private home while the children are still up. Or he can show up at department stores or at special parties in parish halls or school auditoriums. He always has his bag of goodies, and sometimes a lump or two of coal. Today in Poland, it is not uncommon to see this person dressed to look more like Santa Claus, with a red and white suit, stocking cap, and a beard. To Polish children, Saint Nicholas and Santa Claus represent the same person. The Santa Claus costume is just a more modern version of Saint Nicholas' costume. Both bring gifts for the "good little boys and girls." Also more likely today, Saint Nicholas (or Santa Claus) will

parents would tell them that Saint Nicholas brought the presents, and admonished them to remember their morning and evening prayers and to obey their parents. Further admonitions might be tailored to particular children whose behavior needed improvement.

Later on, as the custom took root in Polish towns and villages, a person dressed as Saint Nicholas might ride down the streets in a horse-drawn

Last-minute shopping in Warsaw. This shopper has found a rocking horse for a special child. (left) Shopping for the Wigilia, or Christmas Eve, feast includes choosing plenty of fresh fish. (right) This is a time for fasting, so meat must not be served at the Wigilia table. Fish can make up to twelve courses of the meal.

make a reappearance, visiting children at their homes, on Christmas Eve.

Most children participate in Christmas activities while at school during Advent. Preparations for Saint Nicholas' visit must be completed before his day. Decorations need to be made and hung. Children are taught carols and prayers that they may have to recite for Saint Nicholas. One activity that has become quite popular today is called *Mikołajki*. It is called this because in Polish, Saint Nicholas' name is *Święty Mikołaj*. Mikołajki is similar to a "grab bag." On St. Nicholas Day, each child brings in one small gift to give to a classmate. Who gets whose gift is determined by picking names out of a hat. This assures that each child will receive a gift.

St. Lucy's Day falls on December 13, twelve days before Christmas. Interpreting the celestial bodies on each of these twelve days foretells the weather during each of the months in the coming year.

St. Thomas' Day falls on December 21. An old Polish proverb exhorts, *Od świętego Toma siedź przy piecu doma.* (From St. Thomas on, stay at home near the stove.) It is the first official day of winter and time to stay indoors. Christmas Eve is only three days away, as the final preparations begin.

Wigilia:
A Feast Fit for a King

T he word *Wigilia* (or *Wilia*) comes from the Latin word *vigil*, meaning *watchful* or *awake*. The English word *vigil* comes from the same source. Wigilia is thus a time of watchfulness and expectancy, a time for keeping a vigil. Written with a lower-case letter, wigilia can refer to the eve of any feast. However, with a capital *W*, Wigilia always refers to Christmas Eve.

For many Poles, Wigilia is probably the most important day of the year. It is definitely the biggest family feast day of the year. Wigilia is celebrated with deeply held Christian beliefs and practices. Throughout the centuries, a rich folk tradition has developed around Wigilia, making the day's activities into a feast for the imagination and the soul, as well as for the stomach.

The tradition of keeping a vigil on the day before a holy day dates back to the Old Testament. All preparations for the holy day, all the cleaning and cooking, had to be done by sundown on the day previous. This was done in order to keep the holy day free from work. Not only was this day before the holy day spent in material preparation, it was also necessary to prepare oneself spiritually, by means of fasting and prayer. Wigilia has evolved within the framework of this Old Testament tradition.

Wigilia, or Christmas Eve, is surrounded by religious practices and traditions. But mostly it is filled with plenty of delicious food!

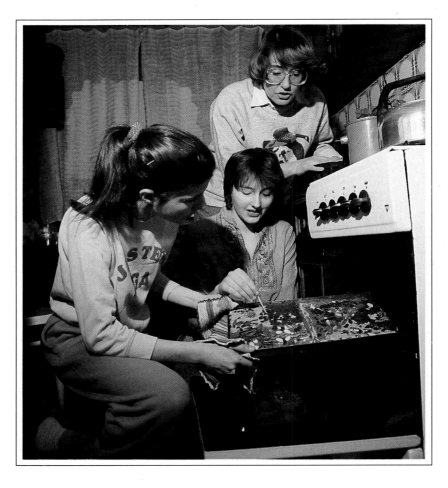

A mother and her daughters prepare one of the desserts for the Wigilia *dinner. A lot of time is spent in the kitchen on this festive day.*

Christmas Eve ushers in the twelve days of Christmas, or Gody, characterized by merry-making and good will. During this time, the old year ends and the new one begins. It is a time to look back and to look forward. Wigilia is the day that initiates Gody and the changes that come with them. As such, Wigilia prefigures these changes. *Jakiś we Wiliją, takiś cały rok.* (The way you conduct yourself on Wigilia—you will conduct yourself throughout the entire year.)

The person who rises early on Wigilia will be wide awake throughout the entire year. It is important that each person rises from bed without having to be awakened by someone else. In villages along the

Baltic coast, it is still customary to give roosters vodka to drink on Christmas Eve. In this way, the farmers thank the roosters for being faithful "alarm clocks." Placing a coin in the wash basin prior to washing oneself will bring health and wealth in the coming year.

The person who is industrious on Wigilia will be full of energy for the next twelve months. Likewise, good health on that day is a sign of more of the same. But the person who cuts him- or herself, or is somehow injured, needs to be watchful over his or her health in the coming year. Sometimes, Polish beliefs seem to be contradictory. In Bielsko Biała (southwest of Kraków), a person who sneezes avoids an

Children play on sleds in the park in an effort to stay out of the way of final preparations for the Wigilia feast.

of the holiest days of the year.

It is also very important not to talk above a whisper in the kitchen while the *babka* is baking. Babka is a type of cake that is made with many egg yolks and yeast in order to rise as high as possible. As such, any sudden noise or loud talk could cause it to collapse in the oven while baking. Of course, there are usually other kinds of cakes and pastries that also need quiet in order to rise properly. On the day before Christmas, kitchens are often "out-of-bounds" for young children. If the children are finished with cleaning, decorating, and other preparations, they may be sent outside to play. This keeps them out of the kitchen and helps them to keep their mind off the presents they will be opening later in the evening.

As so often in their folk calendar, Poles enjoy predicting the weather on Wigilia. A warm Christmas means a cold Easter, or vice versa. *Jeśli w polu czarno, gdy się Chrystus rodzi, to będzie biało na łanie, kiedy Chrystus zmartwychwstanie.* (If the fields are dark when Christ is born, then they will be white when Christ is risen.) And, *Jeśli dzień wigilijny pogodny, roczek będzie urodny.* (If the weather is nice on Wigilia, there will be good weather throughout the year.)

It is not recommended to

early death. However, in Bytom (northwest of Kraków), the number of times a person sneezes during the evening meal will be the number of times he or she will be sick in the new year!

The child who is spanked on Wigilia, it is believed, will need to be disciplined through the whole year. On the contrary, the child who is well behaved and obeys the parents on this day will have no fear of punishment in the coming year. Needless to say, there are many model children in Polish households on Christmas Eve! Children are specifically exhorted not to be noisy on this day. Not only does this ensure a quiet household next year, it shows respect for one lend out something on Wigilia. If this item is important, the lender might be missing it the entire year. Even worse, the act of lending might allow good fortune to leave the home. Washing the laundry on this day, as well as any kind of heavy manual labor, might bring bad luck. The only kind of work that should be done on Wigilia is general house-cleaning, last minute shopping, and of course lots of cooking and baking. The simple act of pounding a nail into the wall might cause a toothache. In rural areas, it is still believed that chopping wood on Wigilia will make for many headaches throughout the year!

Through the centuries, there have been many other beliefs about Christmas Eve held by Poles. Long ago it was believed that well water turned into wine. The farm animals that were present at the birth of the Christ child were able to speak of God's praises on this enchanted evening. Roses bloomed. Even the earth itself could be heard singing . . . though only by the pure of heart. But ours is no longer an enchanted era. Many people today smile at the superstitions of yesterday.

Other traditions involved somewhat complex rituals or simple customs, but were always very meaningful. They ranged from rituals that were performed in the fields or in groves of fruit trees in order to ensure healthy crops in the following year, to customs that concerned the farm animals. However, many of these traditions are rarely observed today, and then only in rural areas.

Throughout Poland, some people still keep a fast on Wigilia. The strict, traditional fast allows for no food to be eaten until the evening meal is taken. And there is no meat allowed this day at all. Although most Poles still abstain from meat, many partake of a small, plain meal once or twice during the day.

A custom that is being increasingly observed in Poland these days is the visiting of family graves during the day on Wigilia. In previous centuries, it was believed that the spirits of ancestors visited their former homes on the day before Christmas. Food was put out for them. Sharp utensils were never brandished in the air, lest the spirits hovering about be injured. All the rooms in the house, whether or not they were being used, were kept warm in case the spirits wanted to stay in them. Old customs sometimes give way to new ones. Lighted votive candles are left on family graves, in much the same way as is done on the Feast of All Souls, November 1. On that night, Polish cemeteries are traditionally ablaze with thousands of individual votive candles. On Christmas Eve, evergreen boughs, or even small evergreen trees are sometimes placed on the graves also.

As the feverish activities and early observances on Wigilia wind down toward late afternoon, an almost enchanted silence tingling with anticipation descends across all of Poland. On farms everywhere, all outside activity ceases. One may see a stray dog or some swirling snow in the streets of smaller towns and villages, but few pedestrians or cars. In the cities, where most people either did not go to work at all or put in only half a day, the streets become nearly deserted. A lone tram car rumbles down ulica Marszałkowska, usually one of Warsaw's busiest thoroughfares.

The Rynek Główny in Kraków, one of the largest town squares in Europe, is wrapped in silence. From one tower of the Kościół Mariacki, St. Mary's Church, on one side of the square, a bugle sounds

Early evening on Wigilia *finds Nowy Swist, one of Warsaw's main streets, nearly deserted. Last minute shoppers catch a bus for home where they will begin the festive celebration.*

the haunting notes of the hejnał . . . a tune cut short by a Tartar's arrow in the Middle Ages . . . in memory of the countless numbers who gave their lives in defense of the homeland. Nearby, on the banks of the Wisła (Vistula), Wawel Castle stands gloomy and immense. It was the royal castle of the Polish kings when Kraków, not Warsaw, was the nation's capital five centuries ago. From the steeples of St. Mary's Church to the towers of Wawel Castle, in Kraków's fairy-tale Stare Miasto, the cobblestoned streets are deserted. The only movement is the rising of smoke out of time-worn chimneys. It is truly a magical evening.

As dusk gathers, a candle is often placed in the front window of the house or apartment. This was once believed to help the spirits of family ancestors to find their way "home" for Wigilia. It is also a sign to a passing stranger who has no place to go that he or she is welcome as an honored guest. No one should be alone on Christmas Eve. Poles have been known for their hospitality for centuries. It is an obligation and a privilege to open one's doors to the weary traveler. *Gość w dom, Bóg w dom.* (A guest in the home is God in the home.)

Underneath the crisp, heavily starched, white linen tablecloth some hay is placed.

In the villages and on the farms, sheaves of grain and straw may be arranged around the room used for the Wigilia meal. Hay and straw are symbols of the birth of the Christ child in a stable. Hay, partially dried grass, clover, or alfalfa, is used as animal feed during the long winter months. Straw, the stalks or stems of grain after drying and threshing, is used as bedding for farm animals.

Stary zwyczaj w tem mają chrześcijańskie domy,
Na Boże Narodzenie po izbie słać słomy,
Że w stajni Święta Panna leżała połogiem.
There is an old custom in Christian homes,
To scatter straw around the house on Christmas,
Because Our Lady lay in a stable, giving birth to her Son.

The longest night and the shortest day of the year is December 21, the winter solstice. On this day, the noonday sun is at its lowest point in the sky. It then begins its slow climb in the heavens until it rises to its highest point on June 21, the summer solstice. On December 21, the days once again start growing longer. On this day in ancient

Preparing the table for dinner includes placing hay under the table-cloth. The hay is a symbol of the birth of the Christ child in a stable.

times, people used to celebrate this "rebirth" of nature, this promise of fertility, this victory of the forces of light over the forces of darkness. What better sign for such a fertility feast than that symbol of the staff of life, sheaves of grain, the source of bread for humans and hay for animals?

The hay is not always placed under the tablecloth today. It is sometimes tied into small bunches resembling miniature sheaves and used as part of the table centerpiece. Every effort is made to ensure that there will be an even number of people at the table on this night. An odd number might signify the death of one of the guests in the coming year. Above all, the number thirteen should be avoided, whether in the number of guests or in the number of courses to be served.

A custom observed throughout Poland is to allow for an extra place setting at the table. The reasons vary from region to region, from city to village, and even sometimes from household to household. There is an extra place setting for that "unexpected guest"— the lonely traveler, who sees the candle burning in the window, or an old family friend or relation, who arrives unannounced. The place setting may be for the Christ child, since the day of the

Second Coming of Christ is unknown and may even fall on Christmas Eve. The setting may be in remembrance of a close relative who passed away recently. Or it may be set to show the spirits of departed ancestors that they are still welcome on Wigilia.

Many Polish homes have an extra place setting in memory of a relative who is far away and not able to be home for Wigilia. Such a place setting is a poignant reminder of how many Poles have migrated in this century to just about every country in the Western world. For many years after World

The table is just about ready for feasting. An extra place (right) *has been set for an "unexpected guest."*

War II, an extra place setting was often set out for the hundreds of thousands of Poles who disappeared or whose family lost track of them during the war. Not officially declared dead, there was always the hope, however slim, that they might someday return to the family home on Wigilia.

In some Polish homes, a candle is lit at dusk in front of a picture of *Matka Boska Częstochowska*, or Our Lady of Częstochowa, also known as the "Black Madonna." The town of Częstochowa lies on the Warta River in south-central Poland. Atop a small hill known as Jasna Góra, or Hill of Light, stands a monastery of the Paulist Fathers founded more than 600 years ago. Containing the sacred picture of the Black Madonna, the monastery's baroque church is the most sacred shrine in all of Poland. Tradition ascribes the painting of this portrait of Mary and the child Jesus to the evangelist Saint Luke. Tradition also tells us that the faces of Mary and Jesus were darkened by smoke from a fire that destroyed the building, but miraculously spared the painting. Hence, the name Black Madonna.

The Mother of God has always been deeply venerated by Poles. Known as *Królowa Korony Polskiej*, Mary is considered to be both the queen of the Polish crown (thus the

A picture of Our Lady of Częstochowa is placed in the window of a Polish home. Christmas lights arranged around it are lit at dusk.

protector of the Polish nation symbolized by the crown) and even Poland's queen herself. She is often addressed by the title Mary, Queen of Poland. During the Feast of the Assumption of Mary (August 15), thousands of Poles go on a pilgrimage, many on foot, to the shrine of Our Lady of Częstochowa. There, they pray to the Black Madonna gazing at the ancient portrait mounted in ebony and silver splendor.

Pomnij, o Panno święta, co Jasnej bronisz Częstochowy, że nigdy nie słyszano, aby, gdy się Polska w potrzebie pod Twoją opiekę uciekała, Twego wspomożenia błagała, od Ciebie opuszczoną była. Remember, Holy Lady, who shines forth from Częstochowa, that whenever Poland in the hour of its need sought your intercession and begged your help, never has she been abandoned by you.

Finally, all is in readiness. The Christmas tree is lit. The presents lie underneath its branches. The dining room is set. The opłatek is on the table. The food is ready to be served. Yet, nothing can begin, until the first star makes its appearance in the heavens. "There in front of them was the star they had seen rising; it went forward and halted over the place where the child was. The sight of the star filled them with delight . . ." (Matthew 2: 9-10). The first star in the heavens on Christmas Eve, the star of Bethlehem, symbols of a continuing tradition . . . But the heavens are sometimes clouded over. The night sky can be obscured by city lights or pollution. In that case, the long-awaited Wigilia supper can begin no later than 6 o'clock.

The family and guests gather for the breaking and sharing of the opłatek. The word *opłatek* is derived from the Latin word *oblatum* which means *sacred bread*. The opłatek is similar to the liturgical wafer that is used as the sacred Host during Mass.

The opłatek is usually a white rectangle 3 by 6 inches (5 by 15 centimeters), with Christmas motifs embossed on one or both sides. The liturgical wafer given at Mass is also white, but it is in the shape of a circle, with Christian symbols embossed on only one side. The traditional opłatek had a Christmas motif on one side and a scene taken from Polish life or folklore on the other side. The latter might include stylized birds, the mountains of southern Poland, or peasant cottages. Today, opłatki are usually embossed on only one side with symbols and images of Christmas.

The breaking and sharing of ceremonial bread is a ritual common to many religious rites. It is a ritual that was adopted by the early Christian communities in the days of the Roman Empire. It is a ritual that is similar to the breaking of the sacred Host during Mass and the distribution of Holy Communion among the faithful. The breaking and sharing of ceremonial bread is the breaking and sharing of opłatek on Wigilia.

The opłatek is a symbol of the strengthening of the bonds between individual family members and between families, villages, towns, and cities, between all Poles—not just those in Poland, but also those scattered throughout the world. As such, it is always sent to family members and close friends who will be absent from the family table on Wigilia. Poles who are thousands of miles away from home, or just across the border, can thus participate in that mystical union that brings all Poles together under one roof on Christmas Eve. This is a feeling quite similar to the

Before the Wigilia *dinner begins, the* opłatek *(Christmas wafer) is broken and shared by all who are present. Best wishes for the coming year are also exchanged.* (above) *The* opłatek *may make up part of the table centerpiece.* (right) *The* opłatek *is a white wafer with a Christmas symbol or image embossed on one side. It symbolizes the strengthening of the bonds between all Polish people.*

togetherness Christmas would bring during the war when Poland was divided. Each year, thousands of opłatki are sent in all directions to the four corners of the earth as Poles exchange Christmas cards with each other.

Before the special dinner begins, the host and hostess each take a piece of opłatek. Turning to each other, one takes a small piece of opłatek from the other, and consumes it. Greetings and best wishes for health and happiness in the coming year are exchanged. If something needs to be forgiven, it is forgiven. If something needs to be forgotten, it is pledged to be forgotten. The past is reconciled. The present

The Wigilia *feast is full of many delicious and varied dishes. It is considered bad luck not to have a taste of each dish.*

is celebrated. The future will always be better. Turning then to everyone else in the room, the same ritual is enacted individually with all those present. Each family member breaks off a piece of opłatek large enough to share in turn with everyone else. The ceremony continues until each person has exchanged opłatek with every other person present.

It is now time to sit down at the table. A brief prayer is usually said by the head of the household and the feasting begins. In some parts of Poland, an odd number of dishes is served, for example, seven, nine, or eleven. But remember, thirteen dishes will bring bad luck. In other parts

of Poland, the meal consists of twelve dishes, symbolizing the twelve apostles. Whatever the number of dishes, it is important to at least try each dish once. *Ile się nie spróbuje, tyle przyjemności w ciągu roku może człowieka ominąć.* (However many dishes are not tasted, a person will lose that much happiness in the coming year.)

The type of foods, the number of dishes, and the order of presentation varies from region to region. What does not vary is the fact that no meat is ever served at a Wigilia supper. Most often, the meal begins with a soup, the most popular being *barszcz.* This is a clear beet broth, usually served with small dumplings known as *uszka* (little ears). The uszka are filled with a mixture of dried mushrooms and spices. Barszcz or a creamed mushroom soup are common in some southern and most eastern sections of Poland. In Silesia and the region around Poznań, however, the soup may be of creamed fish or of almonds cooked with rice, milk, raisins, and honey.

Different kinds of fish prepared in a variety of ways can sometimes comprise up to twelve courses during the Wigilia supper. Herring can be served pickled in a wine sauce or in a cream sauce. It can also be coated with flour and fried. Pike can be boiled and served with a horseradish sauce. It can also be baked with fresh lemon and white wine, or served in aspic. Trout can be steamed in vinegar or baked with mushrooms, breadcrumbs, and cheese. It can also be stuffed with apples, mushrooms, onion, celery, and parsley, and then baked. Carp can be steamed in vinegar or cooked with spices and tomatoes. Sometimes it is boiled and then jellied. Perch is prepared in an egg and olive sauce. Eel is pickled and jellied. Alternatively, most of these fish can be cooked in fresh cream with lemon and butter. Or they can be ground and cooked, seasoned with potato, eggs, apple, and breadcrumbs.

A meatless stew, called *bigos*, or hunter's stew, is one of many side dishes commonly served. The stew is made with sauerkraut, mushrooms, and yellow peas. Other side dishes include cauliflower, served with sautéed breadcrumbs; noodles with poppy seeds or mushrooms; sweet red cabbage with onions; stewed sauerkraut with mushrooms; boiled barley, sautéed with vegetables; and mushrooms mixed with peas or beans. One Polish specialty that is very popular on Wigilia is *pierogi*. Pierogi are dumplings made with noodle dough and stuffed with potato, sauerkraut, mushrooms, cheese, or fruit. They are then boiled, sautéed, or both, and served with sour cream or butter.

Traditionally, alcohol is not to be served at the Wigilia table. Some choose a drink that is made from dried fruit. Other nonalcoholic beverages are also offered.

No Wigilia supper would be complete without a special mixture of dried fruits, called a fruit compote, and a delicious *strucel z makiem*, or poppy-seed coffeecake. Besides the popular poppy-seed filling, this cake can also be made with a nutmeat filling or with walnut or almond fillings. A very traditional dessert that comes from the eastern territo-

ries of prewar Poland is the *kutia*. This is a dish made of cooked, hulled grains sweetened with poppy seeds and honey. Other popular desserts include piernik; babka; nut puddings; cheese cakes; tea cakes; and sometimes even *naleśniki*, Polish crepes filled with cheese or fruit, for those with extra big appetites.

A long-standing Polish tradition is to have the oldest family member present read the Nativity story. Following the story come carols. The more traditional homes tune the violin or the piano for the occasion. More likely, today, a phonograph or the radio may be turned on. But since the introduction of giving presents on Christmas Eve during this century, it has become increasingly difficult to control the anxiousness of young children, to keep their curiosity in check. They are not interested in singing. They are trying to see which presents might be theirs, trying to guess what is inside the wrapped boxes!

The practice of giving presents on Christmas Eve is a fairly recent innovation in Poland. As late as the nineteenth century, only certain areas of the country had a tradition of giving small presents—and then only to children. Most often, these presents were not placed under the Christmas tree, but hidden somewhere in the house. On

After dinner, but before carols and present-opening, the oldest family member reads the Nativity story to the rest of the family. (above) This tree is decorated with lighted candles—the more traditional Christmas tree ornament. The family gathers around the piano to sing kolędy, *or carols. (opposite page)*

After the carols are sung, it is time to exchange gifts. Giving presents on Christmas Eve is a recent tradition in Poland.

farms, they might be hidden in the hayloft. Boys might receive penknives; girls, ribbons or strings of coral beads; small children, cookies, plums in honey, or other sweets. Today, in many Polish households, parents try to bring in a friend or relative dressed up in the traditional St. Nicholas costume, or perhaps in the more modern costume of Santa Claus. He has the children recite a small prayer or asks them about their behavior. Once the child has done this, he or she is given a present. In some homes "a little angel" known as the *aniołek* may be invited in instead of Saint Nicholas.

The presents exchanged in Poland are of a wide variety, like elsewhere in Europe.

Larger, more expensive presents are often given to children. Adults tend to exchange smaller, more personalized presents, sometimes still handmade. The children attack their gifts in much the same way as children in the United States attack their gifts on Christmas morning. With shouts of glee, they play with their new toys, or show off their new clothes. The older children and the adults say "*dziękuję*," or "thank you," to each other. Some return to the dining table; others go into the kitchen. Perhaps another carol or two is sung.

Soon it is time to go to the *Pasterka*, or Shepherd's Mass. This is the midnight Mass, the first Mass celebrated on Christmas Day. Throughout Poland, the streets of villages, towns, and cities become filled with people going to the midnight Mass. And these same streets had been so empty and quiet all evening long! Inside the church, the beloved crèche stands near the altar and all the lights are ablaze. Carols are sung once again. It is customary for many attending midnight Mass to receive Holy Communion. Entire families who have just shared in the Wigilia supper now partake of a spiritual feast. Opłatek earlier in the evening, Holy Communion now at Mass.

After the long midnight Mass, the evening's festivities need not be over. It is still customary for some Poles to go visiting their friends, neighbors, or relations. A young man might visit the home of a young woman whom he likes in a special way. According to tradition, if he takes an apple from the Christmas tree and she does not protest, she has accepted his offer of courtship. Other Poles might visit close friends who live nearby, or exchange visits with their neighbors. Still others might drop in on their uncles or cousins or sisters or nephews. The host will always share the opłatek with the visitors. *Krupnik*, a liqueur made with honey, spices, and alcohol, or some other drink is then offered. This might be followed by hot tea or coffee accompanied by a light snack.

Some brave souls might even be out singing carols during these, the early hours of Christmas morning. This practice is more common in the villages than in the larger towns or cities. Nonetheless, the carolers, can expect to receive a few pennies for their vocal efforts. Older carolers might receive a glass of krupnik; the younger ones, some sweets. But soon, it is time to go to bed. It has been a long and exciting day. And more feasting lies ahead. In fact, now begin Gody, the twelve days of Christmas, days of friendship and good cheer.

At the Pasterka, *or Shepherd's Mass, parishioners receive Holy Communion. This is only the first of three Masses that will be celebrated on Christmas.*

Gody: The Twelve Days of Christmas

fter all the ritual and festivities of Wigilia, Christmas Day itself seems rather anticlimactic. Nonetheless, this is the anniversary of the first day in the life of Jesus, and it is a very holy day.

The Mass at midnight is the Shepherd's Mass. The Mass said at dawn is known as the Angel's Mass. The third Mass on Christmas is known as the Mass of the Three Kings. These are three different Masses, each with its own prayers and scriptural readings. There is only one set of prayers and scriptural readings for the daily Mass said on each of the other days in the church calendar. Pious Poles may still attend each of the three Masses of Christmas. After Mass, it is customary to view the crèche, which stands to one side of the main altar. It may even be large enough to cover one of the side altars.

Christmas Day is spent with one's immediate family. Gatherings of the extended family and visiting with friends still usually wait until the following day, St. Stephen's Day. According to custom, the main meal of the day is a midafternoon dinner. Although there is no set number of courses and no special types of food as on Wigilia, the fast is over and there is plenty of meat.

Leaving church after the Angel's Mass on Christmas morning. It is now time to go home and celebrate this most sacred of holy days with close family members.

Families going to Mass fill the streets of villages, towns, and cities.

A very popular dish in many Polish homes on Christmas is the hunter's stew. A meatless variety may have been served on Christmas Eve. But on Christmas Day, the stew may contain combinations of pork, veal, beef, and lamb. A traditional blend of meats combines roast pork, ham, and sausage. Venison or the meat of any wild animal can also be added. The other ingredients include raw cabbage, sauerkraut, onions, dried mushrooms, prunes, and various spices. This is a thick, hearty stew that is made several days earlier and then reheated on Christmas Day. In fact, it tastes even better after being allowed to sit for a while; the flavors blend together much more fully. The stew is also a popular dish on Christmas Day because it only

needs to be reheated. It is customary to do as little work as possible in the kitchen on Christmas Day.

Baked ham and Polish sausage are also very popular at the dinner table on Christmas. Various side dishes can be prepared. These often include dried mushrooms, which are used in various holiday preparations. A loaf of hearty Polish rye bread can accompany the meal, or perhaps a braided, or egg-twist, bread. This is a lighter bread made with white flour and extra egg yolks. It may have raisins or be otherwise slightly sweetened. Whatever kind of bread accompanies the meal, the centuries-old tradition of making the sign of the cross on the bread with the tip of the knife before slicing it will be upheld.

In Poland, Christmas is the first day of Gody, the twelve days of Christmas. These days will be filled with feasting and harmony. According to tradition, the weather and other occurrences during each of these twelve days predict how each of the twelve months of the coming new year may turn out. A similar type of folklore surrounds the twelve days between St. Lucy's Day (December 13) and Christmas. Christmas can prefigure January, St. Stephen's Day (December 26) February, and so on. The predictions can even be taken a step further. The morning's weather can prefigure what the beginning of the month will be. The afternoon's weather will parallel the middle of the month, and the evening's weather, the end of the month. Although few Poles believe in such fortune-telling anymore, they may still try to predict the weather or other events in the coming months out of "curiosity."

There was once an interesting means by which the weather for the coming months could be predicted during these days between Christmas and the Epiphany, or the Feast of the Three Kings (January 6). A dozen onion peels, each representing one of the months of the year, would be lined up on a window sill. The peels were then topped with salt, from left to right. On the morning of each of the twelve days, one of the onion peels was closely observed. If the salt was dry, the corresponding month would also be dry. If the salt was damp, the corresponding month would have rain. Such observations lack the backing of science, but they were colorful and imaginative ways to pass the time during the long winter months.

The Feast of Saint Stephen falls on December 26, often called *drugi dzień świąt*, or the second Christmas. It is another important day and is observed by most as an official day off from work. This was, and still often is, the day for visiting friends and more distant family relations. The harmony and good cheer that began on Christmas with the immediate family now begin to ripple outward to include aunts, uncles, cousins, family friends, old friends, any and all friends. The poppy-seed coffeecake and honey spice cake are now cut up into many slices. Hot tea and krupnik are served to the guests. The festivities of Gody continue merrily forward.

Traditionally, the *szopki* (live or static Christmas crèche scenes) and *kolędnicy* (carolers) made their appearance on St. Stephen's Day. The customs and traditions that surround this occasion will all be explained on pages 59-64. An old tradition that has not been observed on this day for a long time is the throwing of oats or peas at the parish priest or the neighbors or one's friends. Such a tradition was done in memory of Saint Stephen, who was stoned to death.

In some parts of Poland, the Feast of Saint John the Apostle (December 27) is considered to be *trzecie święto Bożego Narodzenia*, or the third Christmas, a day that was set aside for the blessing of wine. According to tradition, a pagan priest challenged Saint John to prove the superiority of his God by drinking from a poisoned cup, which Saint John did without harm. It was once customary for adults and older children to drink a glass of blessed wine on this day. Even little children were given a spoonful of the wine.

New Year's Eve is sometimes called St. Sylvester's Day, or just Sylvester, in Poland and other European countries, because it coincides with the Feast of Saint Sylvester. This saint, pope from 314 to 335, was the center of many legends during the Middle Ages. For example, it was widely believed that Sylvester cured the Emperor Constantine of leprosy and stories were told of his imprisoning a dragon.

New Year's Eve parties did not enter into Polish tradition until fairly recently. Noisy celebrations accompanying the end of the old year and greeting the beginning of the new began in

Italy. The custom caught on in Poland during the nineteenth century. At the time, the start of the new year was much more celebrated than the end of the old. Today, the practice of throwing grand balls on New Year's Eve is still not widely known in Poland. Most Poles spend the evening celebrating with family or friends at parties usually given in private homes. Poles rarely spend this evening alone. If there is no party with the family, then there is a party thrown by friends or neighbors. The traditional greeting for New Year's is *"Do siegu roku"* ("Good fortune in the New Year"). And the answer is *"Nawzajem"* ("Same to you"). Another popular greeting is *"Szczęsliwego nowego roku"* ("Happy New Year").

Niech tu Boskie Miłosierdzie w tym domu ostanie.
Niech to Jezus i Maryja w tym domu przebywa.
Niech tu pszeniczka i żytko, na ten Nowy Rok wszyćko!
May the love of God rest within these walls.
May Jesus and Mary come and always dwell in this home.
May there be plenty of wheat and rye,
In the New Year plenty of everything!

In the church calendar, New Year's Day is the octave of Christmas, the eighth day of religious observance after Christmas. New Year's Day is also the Feast of the Circumcision of Our Lord. This is the day on which the Baby Jesus was circumcised in the Temple of Jerusalem, presented to God, and given the name of Jesus.

In some areas of Poland, the New Year's Day tradition of playing tricks on friends or family members is still very much alive. This tradition is somewhat like April Fool's Day in America. Stealing an article of clothing, done in jest, brings good fortune during the coming year. If a girl steals from a boy, she can hold it for ransom. Many such folk customs and superstitions still survive in parts of Poland. Though rarely believed in, they may still be traditionally observed. The person who rises early on New Year's Day will be an early riser throughout the year. The person who places the right foot on the floor before the left when getting out of bed in the morning will enjoy great fortune in the coming year. Sometimes, small rolls are baked in the shapes of

Kolędnicy, or carolers, gather around the szopka, or crèche, at their church in Białystok. In many churches it is traditional to sing carols before, during, and after Mass.

rings, crosses, and babies. They are then hidden on the dinner table, at the place settings of the young boys and girls in the family. The ring means, naturally, marriage. The one who finds a cross will be a priest or a nun. And the baby means a baby will arrive soon, or, by extension, that a wedding will take place.

In the Mazowsze region in central Poland, little figures made of bread dough are still baked for New Year's Day. They take the forms of animals and birds. Long ago, this was believed to ensure a plentiful supply of farm animals in the coming year. Small rolls baked in the forms of wild animals promised that the forests would have much game for hunting in the coming year. Though no longer baked for these reasons, the little rolls are still made—mostly to delight the children.

In the Podhale region of southern Poland, a similar tradition was once widely popular. Godparents would visit with their godchildren and present them with small rolls in the shape of farm animals. These were meant to bring good luck in the coming year. Sometimes, pieces of animal-shaped dough would be arranged on a larger ring of dough and baked as one large loaf of bread. One animal would stand behind the other, as if moving in a circle around

the ring. The arrangement symbolized the cyclical turn of the seasons: Spring follows winter, then summer follows spring, and so on.

In regions along the Baltic coast, people would bake filled doughnuts called *pączki,* similar to a Bismarck. These treats were a sign that the coming year would be equally as prosperous as the dough-nuts were tasty. Throughout Poland, in general, bread or bread rolls were often left on the dining table all day long on New Year's Day. This was done in order to symbolize a sufficient supply of this staff of life in the coming year.

The twelve days of Christ-mas come to an end on the Feast of the Epiphany, January 6. An ancient Christian holy day, the Epiphany is older even than Christmas. The word *epiphany* comes from a Greek word meaning *to show.* An epiphany is thus an appear-ance or a manifestation of a deity.

Starting in the 200's, the baptism of the Lord was com-memorated on January 6. By the 400's, the Epiphany of the Lord was commemorated in the universal church calendar. The Epiphany recalled not only the appearance of God in the baptism at the Jordan, but also His birth in the Bethlehem stable. It also commemorated His manifestation to the three kings and His revealing of

Himself through the first miracle at Cana. At the same time, the popularity of December 25 as the day of the birth of Jesus was on the rise. Eventually in the Western (Latin) Church, January 6 became established as the Feast of the Three Kings. In the Eastern (Orthodox) Church, January 6 became established as the feast day in commemoration of the Lord's baptism.

Nowhere in the New Testament are the number or the names of the three kings ever mentioned. In fact, they are not even called kings, rather the Magi, or wise men. But three gifts were brought, so perhaps there were three of them. They became kings as the legends around the birth of Christ grew in the first several centuries of our era. By sometime in the 500's, they were beginning to be known by the names that would become traditional: Caspar (or Gaspar), Melchior, and Balthasar. The Gospels do mention, however, that the three gifts were gold, frankincense, and myrrh.

It was once traditional in Poland to bring rings of gold,

St. Stephen's Day (December 26) is still a very holy holiday and is traditionally spent visiting with friends and distant relatives. This family, living in the mountains, has decided to use the horse and sleigh for visiting.

or even of silver, to church on January 6 to be blessed. This custom is still sometimes observed. Frankincense and myrrh, both used as a fragrant incense, are also blessed on that day. In addition, water is blessed on January 6 in memory of the baptism of Christ. The resulting holy water has various uses in Catholic ritual.

On Epiphany (January 6), or the Feast of the Three Kings, chalk is used to inscribe the letters K, M, *and* B *on the doorframe of the main entrance of the home. The letters stand for the initials of the three kings. Between each letter a cross is drawn. The two digits of the century are written to the left of the letters and the two digits of the year to the right of the letters.*

A custom still very much alive in Poland is the inscribing of the letters *K, M,* and *B*—or sometimes the letters *C, M, B*—on the doorframe above and inside the main entrance to the house or apartment. *K* is more often used rather than *C* because the Polish version of Caspar is Kacper. First, chalk is taken to Mass on the morning of the sixth, where it is blessed. The blessed chalk is then used to inscribe the letters. The letters are separated by small crosses. The year is also inscribed, usually the two digits of the century to the left of the letters and the two digits of the year to the right of the letters. The letters are allowed to remain throughout the year until they are cleaned off in preparation for a

new inscription on the next Epiphany.

The letters over the door of a home signify that here lives a Christian family. This practice is an echo of the blood of the lamb that was used to mark the doors of the Israelites during the Passover in Egypt. When God's destroying angel came during the night, he passed over the homes of all those who had this sacrificial blood on their doorjambs. In a similar way, Poles hope that evil and sickness will by-pass the homes of those who have the mark of the three kings over their doors.

As on virtually every day of these holidays, there is a proverb that predicts the weather. *Na Trzy Króle słońce świeci, wiosna do nas pędem leci.* (If the sun shines on the Feast of the Three Kings, then spring is rushing toward us.) There is also the tradition of baking a pastry or cake with a single almond in it. Whoever gets the piece with the almond will be married during *zapusty,* the carnival time just before Lent begins.

A unique and chilling ceremony was once enacted by Orthodox Christians in Poland's eastern territories. On January 6, they commemorated the baptism of Jesus in the following fashion: A hole was dug in the ice over a frozen pond, where a provisional altar was set up. From the local church, a procession of priests and laity wound its way to the pond. With banners and flags flying and icons shimmering in the sunlight, the water was blessed with many a prayer and song. Then, near the end of the ceremony, a young man would strip himself and jump through the hole in the ice into the pond. After dunking his head three times, he emerged from the icy water steaming and red. Throwing on his boots and greatcoat, he would rush back to the warmth of his home and a glass of vodka. Next, other men repeated this ritual in honor of the Lord's baptism. The icy plunge also had the function, according to tradition, of insuring the health of these men for the coming year.

In the calendar of the Western Church, the baptism of the Lord is celebrated on the first Sunday after the Feast of the Three Kings. This Sunday ends the liturgical observance of the Christmas holiday. Many Poles observe the end of the Christmas season on the Feast of the Three Kings. January 6 had ended the period of good will and feasting of Gody. However, other Poles, especially those living in rural areas, continue to celebrate the Christmas season through February 2, the Feast of the Purification of Our Lady, also known as Candlemas Day. Occurring forty days after Christmas, Candlemas Day observes the purification of the Virgin Mary and the presentation of the Baby Jesus to the

Temple. Most people attending Mass on this day bring with them a candle to be blessed. After the Mass, the candle is brought home and kept there for a year, until the next Candlemas Day. The candles recall the lights of Christmas. February 2 is thus the official ending of the Christmas season for many Poles. There are no more rituals to enact, no more special foods to sample, no more holiday predictions to make, no more customs to keep, no more traditions to observe—at least until next November, when the Christmas festivities start all over again.

This beautifully carved scene of the presentation of the three kings is part of the Mariacki Altar inside St. Mary's Church in Kraków. Wit Stwosz created this masterpiece which consists of panels depicting various scenes. The dimensions of the altar are 36 by 43 feet (11 by 13 meters), making it one of the largest altars in Europe.

Szopki:
Fairy-Tale Stables

Mention the words *Christmas manger* or *Christmas crèche* to most people, and they think of a tableau of the Nativity: a model of the Bethlehem stable filled with figurines of the Baby Jesus, Mary, Joseph, the shepherds, perhaps the three kings, and the animals associated with the Nativity setting. But mention the equivalent Polish words to Poles—*żłobek* and *jasełka/szopka* (plural forms: *jasełka/szopki*)—and they think of puppet shows, a portable marionette theater, even live theater; carols, singing, laughing, inspiration, drama mingled with comedy; the Holy Family, Polish shepherds and kings, farmers, soldiers, and students; angels, death, the devil, and King Herod; Bethlehem stables that look like fairy-tale castles and shimmering cathedrals; religious scenes which can also be historical pageants, morality lessons, and occasions for wry, even sarcastic, humor.

The Christmas crèche is part of the common heritage of all Christians. The Polish szopka is unique to Poland, especially in Kraków where special szopki contests and exhibitions are held.

Winners of the crèche competition in Kraków hold up their prized masterpiece. The design of the crèches entered in the contest has evolved from a simple manger scene in a stable to beautiful works of art having the appearance of a temple or a church.

A performance of the Nativity story at the Warsaw theater shows what the early jasełka*, or crèche scenes, may have looked like when live actors began taking the place of static figures many years ago. Such crèche scenes took place inside churches.*

The custom of putting together a Christmas crèche began with Saint Francis of Assisi, who according to tradition organized the first Nativity tableau in the year 1223. From Italy, this new form of education and edification reached across the Alps, popularized by the sermonizing Franciscans. The earliest evidence of a crèche in Poland can be found in St. Andrew's Church in Kraków. Two wooden, polychromed figures stand in a fourteenth century Gothic stable.

The early jasełka, or crèches, were quite simple and portable. They had a back wall, two side walls, and a thatched roof resting on four poles or pillars. The front was open. The wooden or clay figures were often moved around to display different scenes from the early life of the Christ child. These scenes might be of the Nativity, the visit of the three kings, or the flight into Egypt. The jaselka remained on display from Christmas until Candlemas Day, February 2. Eventually, monks took on the roles of all the figurines, except for the Baby Jesus and the animals. Little by little, instructional dialogue was added. For example, the priest would ask, "Where are you going?" And a monk dressed as one of the three kings would answer, "To pay homage to the newborn king."

Thus, the jasełka developed and grew for three or four centuries. The monks were replaced or joined by the peasants from the villages and the tradesmen of the towns. Students, artisans, soldiers, and members of the nobility also took turns. Slowly, new characters were added: figures out of history or local life; allegorical figures like the devil and death; and other figures from the Bible, such as Herod. Even the setting would change. The Bethlehem stable might become a room in a manor house or a square in a village.

Not all jasełka were peopled by live actors. Some jasełka were filled with small figurines, sometimes even hundreds of them. Besides the traditional Biblical figures, there appeared farmers driving their wagons, nobles on horseback, soldiers marching in formation, peasant women in their Sunday finery, and guilds of artisans. Whole armies materialized to accompany the three kings, riding on camels, elephants, and horses.

By the eighteenth century, these figures were being made movable. Puppets, manipulated by strings, were replacing the static figurines, a practice adapted from the French marionette theaters. By this time, comedy in the form of rustic humor or broad farce had made its entrance on the religious stage of the szopka, as the jasełka was now called. The show may have begun with the puppets dressed as two drunken peasants fighting. The innkeeper's daughter would be dancing with a suitor when suddenly the devil puppet would pop up out of the floor of the theater and drag them both down to hell. Or the death puppet could be seen dancing with the devil, and then fighting with him.

Still all going on in a church, the puppet theater was supposed to be a Nativity scene. The spectators would crowd and push forward to see the performances better. More and

more often, fights would break out. There would be screams and laughter. Eventually, church authorities began to realize that these szopki had really gotten out of hand.

Inevitably, by the mid-1700's, these szopki were banned from churches. Both the shows with live actors and the puppet shows now passed under the control of lay people.

Over the next two centuries, the live-actor szopki became traveling shows. The players moved from home to home or village to village during the holidays, usually beginning on St. Stephen's Day (December 26). Often accompanied by the parish priest, they would make brief dramatic presentations, sing carols, and accept payment in food and drink and sometimes a few pennies. The priest would usually be given gifts of a more substantial nature, to take back with him to the parish larder or to the church.

The following scenario was typical during the nineteenth

After the mid-1700's, live-actor szopki, *or crèche scenes, were banned from churches because they had become too noisy and disruptive. Over the next two centuries, the* szopki *became traveling shows. Here a group of carolers carries on that tradition. The "devil" leads the group with "death," "King Herod," and a host of extras following.*

The tradition of live-actor szopki*, once performed by traveling carolers in the villages of Poland, is kept alive today in schools by students who reenact them. Here students have brought together the traditional characters of the* szopka*, such as the devil and angels, with Saint Nicholas. The class is picking names for an activity called* Mikołajki. *By picking names, each student knows to whom his or her gift should be given.*

century: The players, or carolers, would descend on a farmhouse or a manor house and politely ask if they could entertain the family with drama and song. The players included one dressed as King Herod in a long coat, bearded, and with a crown on his head. Another dressed as the devil with a long tail and horns. Then there was "death" dressed in a white robe (often a blanket) and carrying a scythe. A host of extras (angels, shepherds, attendants) accompanied the procession. The parish priest usually came along as a chaperon since the players were often teen-agers. The head of the household would invite them in. In one of the larger rooms, the furniture would be moved against one wall to make space for this little bit of theater. Then the presentation would begin.

First, some carols. Then the dramatic spectacle itself. Herod begins his evil monologue on the massacre of the Innocents. The angels sing the glory of God. Death moves menacingly in the background. The shep-

herds seem confused. The devil steps forward and demands the soul of the king. The shepherds cower in fear. The angels keep singing. But all evildoers must go to the devil. Shouts, screams, confusion, maybe a few chuckles from the adults in the audience. Death moves up behind the monarch and waves his scythe at him. The crown falls off. As Herod lowers his head into his hands, the devil shouts in triumph, *"Królu Herodzie, za twe grzechy, za twe zbytki, chodź do piekła, boś ty brzydki."* ("King Herod, for your wickedness and the sins you have committed, come with me to hell, because you're deplorable.")

Now the players sing more carols, joined this time perhaps by those in the audience. They end their singing with the following song.

Winszujemy wam, panie
   gospodarzu,
Tym Panem Jezusem
W żłóbeczku na sianeczku.
Winszować nie przestaniemy,
Póki kolędy nie dostaniemy!
We greet you, o master of the
   house,
In the name of Jesus
Who lies in a manger.
We will not stop greeting you,
Until we receive our due!

After the players have received some Christmas cakes and perhaps a few pennies, maybe even a glass or two of krupnik, they sing again.

Za kolędę dziękujemy.
Zdrowia, szczęścia wam
  życzymy.
Żebyście długo żyli,
A po śmierci w niebie byli.
We thank you for your
  generosity.
And wish you health and good
  fortune.
May you live a long life,
And after death find yourselves
  in heaven.

Although such szopki are rarely performed anymore in such a fashion, their memory is kept alive by schoolchildren who sometimes reenact them. And of course, older Poles have heard and read about these szopki many times during their childhood. In recent years, there has been a renewed interest in the ancient and venerable tradition of this type of szopka.

The puppet-show szopka has also survived to the present day. It is more widely known and more popular than the live shows. The annual competition in Kraków also includes these szopki.

After the puppet-show szopki were barred from the churches along with the live-

Figurines depicting characters from Polish history and folklore are lined up outward from the first floor of one of the crèches.

show szopki in the eighteenth century, the former evolved into true products of Polish folk art. Throughout that century, the szopka as a simple Nativity scene became more and more popular in the homes of Polish nobles and other Poles living in the cities. These crèches were often imported from France or from Italy. In the meantime, native artisans were making szopki with distinctively Polish architectural motifs. The puppets for these szopki wore native costumes. The shepherds were dressed as Polish farmers and the three kings were dressed as some of the kings from Poland's past.

Each region of Poland developed a szopka with its own unique characteristics. Warsaw's szopki were especially known for their secular architectural motifs. The szopki often resembled castles, town halls, or palaces. But it was in

Kraków that a szopka was developed which became so uniquely its own that there is no other like it in the world.

By the first half of the nineteenth century, several characteristics defined the szopka's general shape. The stable with the Nativity scene was flanked by two towers. The stable's thatched roof was covered by a second story, which also extended left and right over the towers, doubling their height. A dome, or a central tower, rose from the middle of the second story. The two towers were again extended upward and culminated in steeples. The entire front of the szopka had the appearance of a temple or a church.

Eventually, the two towers would resemble the two towers of the Church of St. Mary in Kraków. If there was a central dome, it might resemble the Renaissance dome of the Zygmunt (Sigismund) Chapel in the cathedral atop Kraków's Wawel Hill. Together, the two towers and the dome, or the three towers (if there was no dome), eventually became a third story.

By the end of the nineteenth century, the stable had been moved up to the second story. This meant the entire first floor could then contain a tableau of figurines from Polish history and folklore. A proscenium might extend outward from the middle of the first floor.

And across its stage, a parade of up to dozens of exquisitely carved puppets would dance. Or dozens of figurines would stand at silent attention, the threesome of Herod, the devil, and death sometimes making up the center of the tableau.

The Ethnographic Museum in Kraków has many beautiful szopki on permanent display. Each year, there is a contest for new szopki, which are still being made by Polish craftsmen and artisans. Sometimes even whole families get together to build a szopka for the contest. Perhaps there is no other activity that better symbolizes the care, craftsmanship, and family tradition that mark everything else about the Christmas season in Poland!

A father and daughter work diligently on the crèche that they will enter in the annual competition. A lot of time and energy go into making these splendid feasts for the eyes.

Polish Ornaments

World ornament

Materials
construction paper
scissors
needle and thread

Instructions

1. Trace circles A, B, and C, including the cut lines, to make a tracing pattern. Use this pattern as a guide when cutting the construction paper.

2. Cut the circles out of construction paper. Each circle may be a different color. Be sure to also cut along the cut lines.

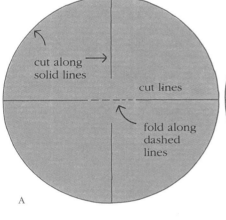

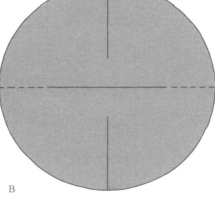

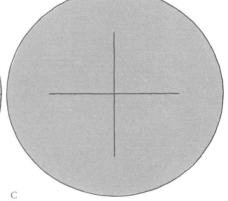

A

B

C

3. Fold circle A in half and insert through the center slot of circle B. Unfold circle A.

4. Fold circles A and B so that the cut slots line up. Insert the two folded circles through circle C.

5. Gently unfold the circles and "lock" them into place so they make a ball. To make a hanger loop, bring a needle and thread through the edge of one of the circles.

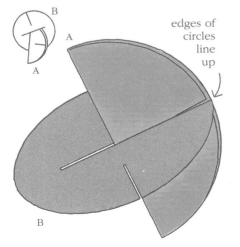

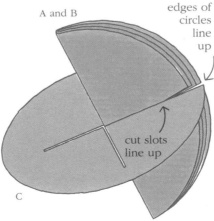

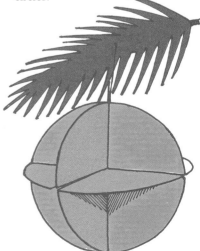

Porcupine ornament

Materials

heavy-duty aluminum foil

scissors

sharp pencil

heavy thread (about 8 inches in length for each ornament)

embroidery needle

cardboard (like that of a shoebox)

Instructions

1. Trace the circle on a piece of paper, including the eight cut lines, to make a cutting pattern. Use this pattern as a guide when cutting the aluminum foil.

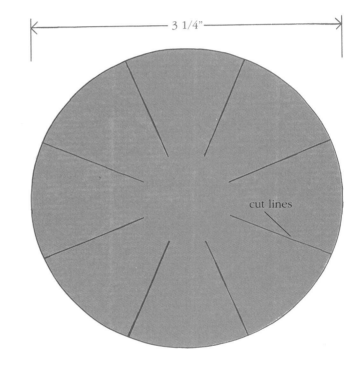

3 1/4"

cut lines

2. Cut 12 circles of foil. Cut each circle separately or stack sheets of foil with tissue paper between each, and cut several circles at once. Be sure to also cut along the cut lines.

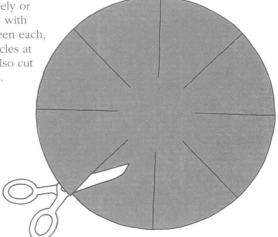

3. Wrap a segment of one of the circles around the tip of the sharpened pencil to form a cone. The foil will hold this cone shape. Repeat this step for each segment of all 12 circles.

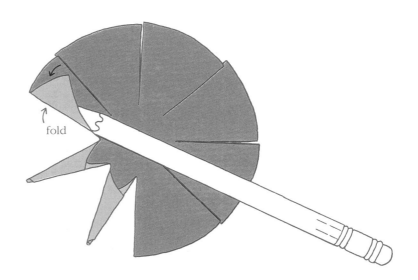

fold

4. Cut a 1-inch circle out of the cardboard.

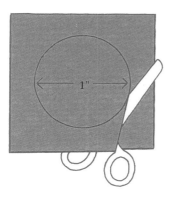

1"

5. To assemble the ornament, bring a needle and thread through the center of six of the circles. Each circle should face the same way. Continue to thread through the center of the cardboard and then through the remaining six circles, making sure that the last six circles face the opposite direction from the first six. Bring both ends of the thread together and tie tightly, near the edge of the cardboard circle. The points will spread naturally into a ball. Use the remaining thread as a tree hanger.

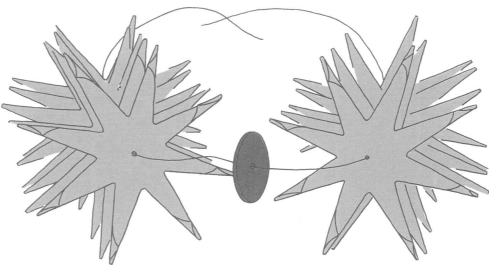

Eggshell pitcher ornament

Materials

large white egg

scissors

colored construction paper

glue

needle

toothpick

Instructions

1. To begin, the contents of an egg will have to be emptied. Gently make a small hole at the top and at the bottom of an egg. Use a sewing needle to start the hole. The hole then can be made larger by working a toothpick back and forth in the hole, but do not make it too large. The toothpick will break the egg yolk, making it easier to blow it out of the egg.

2. Over a bowl, blow into one end of the egg. The inside of the egg will come out slowly—be patient! Rinse the inside of the eggshell with water.

Pattern I, Top

Pattern II, Spout

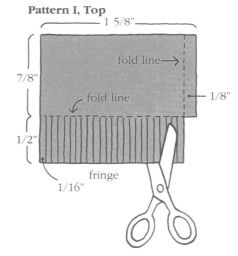

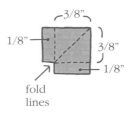

3. Using construction paper, cut out the pieces for the top (pattern I) and the spout (pattern II). Use the same color paper for both pieces. On the top piece, draw cut lines 1/2 inch from the bottom and 1/16 inch apart as shown in pattern I. Cut along the cut lines, making a fringe.

4. Roll the top piece into a cylindrical shape and glue the edge as shown in figure A.

5. When the glue has dried, cut a 3/8-inch notch at the top of the cylinder (figure B). Fold back slightly the edges to create an opening.

6. Take the spout piece and put glue on the outer edges. The outer edges of the spout should touch the inner edges of the opening made on the cylinder as shown in figure C. Glue into place.

Figure A

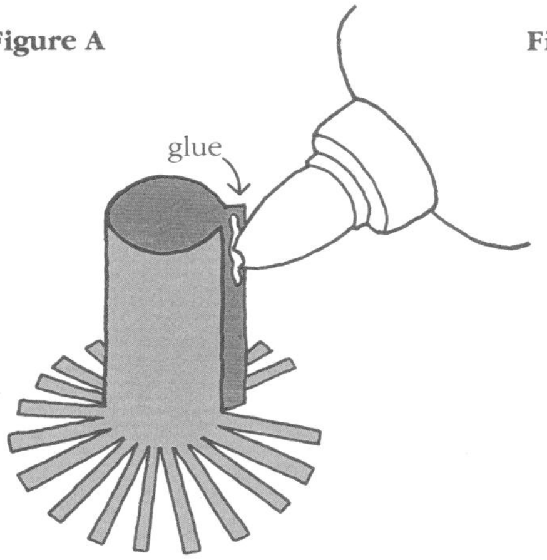

glue

Figure B

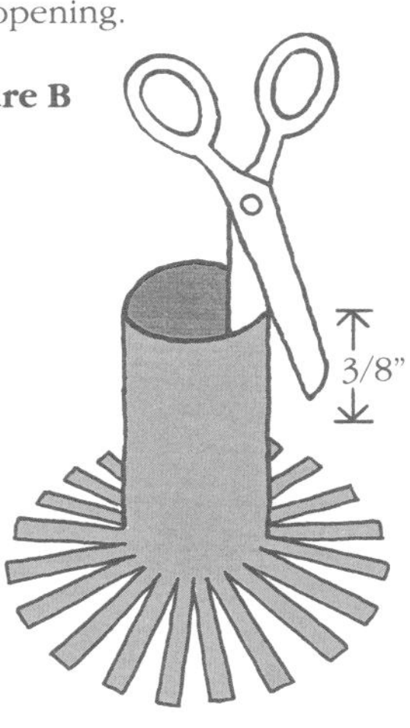

3/8"

Figure C

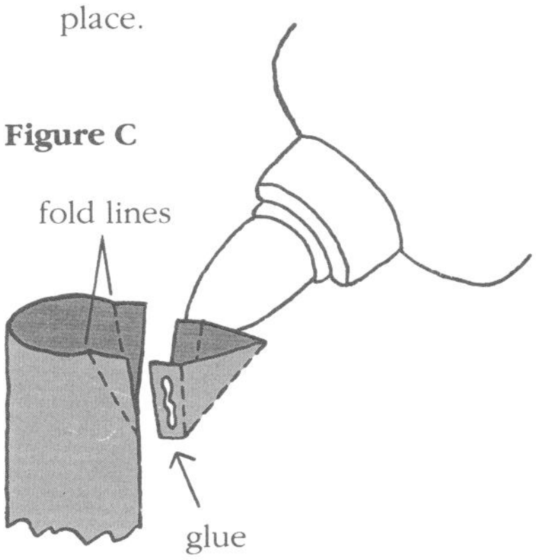

fold lines

glue

Pattern III, Base

fringe

1/16"

1/2"

3/8"

fold line   fold line

1/8"

3 3/8"

7. Cut out the base (pattern III) for the pitcher. On the base, draw cut lines 1/2 inch from the top and 1/16 inch apart. Cut along the lines, making a fringe. Roll the base piece into a cylindrical shape and glue the edge.

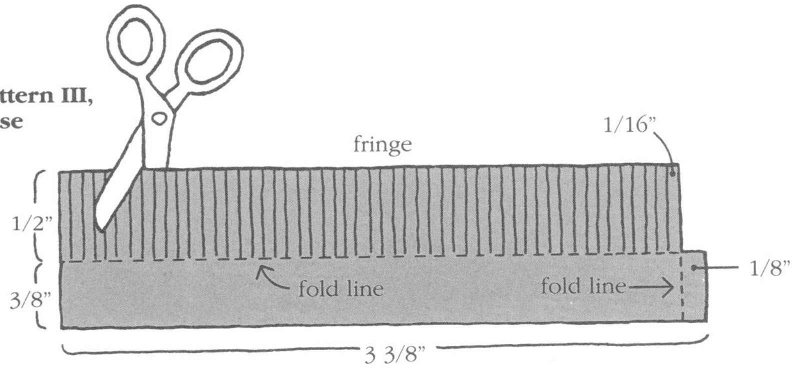

8. Glue the fringe of the top piece (with spout) onto the smaller end of the egg. Glue the fringe of the base piece onto the larger end of the egg.

9. Cut out the handle (pattern IV) for the pitcher. Glue the handle to the pitcher as indicated in figure D.

Figure D

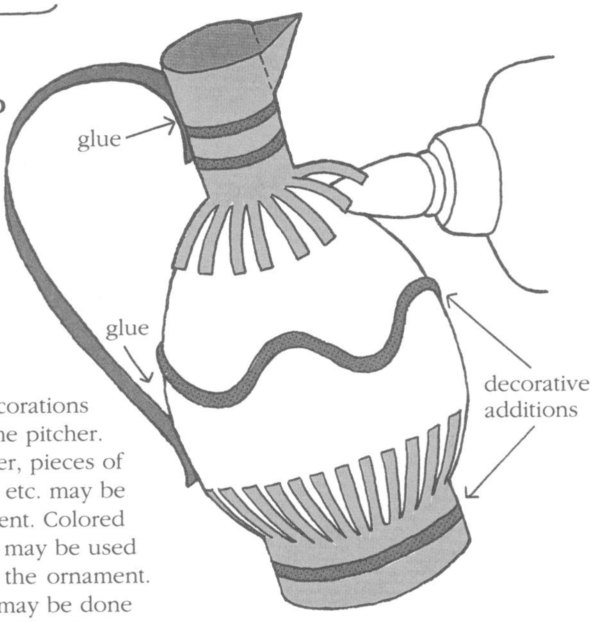

glue

glue

decorative additions

10. If desired, other decorations may be added to the pitcher. Colored string, glitter, pieces of construction paper, etc. may be glued to the ornament. Colored markers or crayons may be used to draw designs on the ornament. A variety of things may be done to make each eggshell pitcher unique.

Pattern IV, Handle

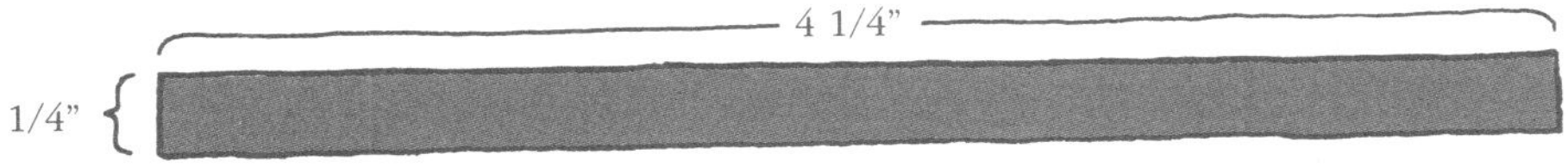

4 1/4"

1/4"

Geometric ornament

Materials

several thin, white, plastic
  drinking straws

yarn

scissors

needle, blunt point

Instructions

1. Cut 30 pieces of drinking straws,
   1 1/2 inches in length each. Cut a
   length of yarn approximately 80
   inches long. Thread the yarn
   through a blunt needle (a needle-
   point needle is suggested).

Figure A   16" of yarn left
                at end
                            first knot   →

shaded straws indicate
your first triangle

2. Thread one straw piece so that it
   is 16 inches away from the end of
   the yarn. Thread two more straw
   pieces and tie a knot to form the
   first triangle (figure A). Thread
   two more straw pieces and tie a
   knot to form a second triangle.
   Repeat until there are nine
   triangles (figure B).

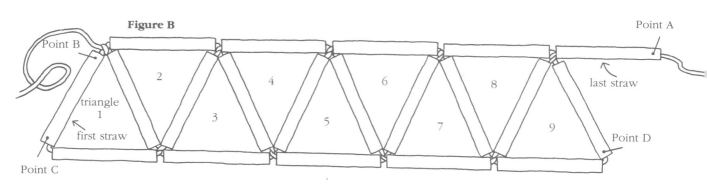

Figure B   Point A

Point B

triangle
1

first straw

Point C

2   4   6   8

3   5   7   9

last straw

Point D

3. Thread one straw piece and draw it around to the very first piece, point A to point B (figure C). Tie a knot. Pass the yarn through the first straw piece and connect the third side of the triangle by tying a knot where point C and D meet (figure C). There will now be a ring of triangles.

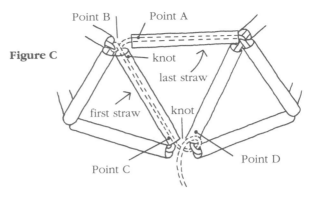

Figure C

Point B

Point A

knot

last straw

first straw

knot

Point C

Point D

Note: dashed lines show how the yarn is passed through the straw pieces and knotted to make the ring of triangles.

4. To form the top of the ornament, thread two straws onto the remaining yarn where the last joining knot was made, *a* in figure D. Make a knot at *b*. Pass the yarn through straw, exiting at *c*. Thread one straw piece and make a knot at *d*. Add another straw piece and make a knot at *e*. Pass yarn through straw, exiting at *f*. Add one more straw piece and make a knot at *d*. After the final knot is made, form a hanger loop with the remaining yarn and knot. Cut off the unused yarn.

Figure D

d

a

b

c

e

f

5. Repeat step 4 with the remaining five straws to form the bottom of the ornament. Use the 16 inches of yarn measured off at step 2. After the final knot is made cut off the remaining yarn.

hanger loop

Polish Carols

Gloria, Gloria, in Excelsis Deo

Latin Doxology (Luke 2:14)   Original Composition by Rose Polski Anderson

Glo - ri - a, Glo - ri - a, in ex - cel - sis De - o.

Glo - ri - a, Glo - ri - a, in ex - cel - sis De - o.

Glo - ri - a, Glo - ri - a, in ex - cel - sis De - o.

The carols on pages 72-76 are from,
Treasured Polish Christmas Customs and
Traditions.
© 1972 by Polanie Club, Inc., 643 Madison
N.E., Minneapolis, Minnesota 55413.
Reproduced with permission.

72

Lullaby, Sweet Jesus Lulajże, Jezuniu

English version-Evelyn Cieslak
Music Arr.-Rose Polski Anderson

Andantino

1. Lul - la - by, sweet Je - sus, pearl ve - ry pre - cious,
Lu - laj - że, Je - zu - niu, mo - ja pe - reł - ko,

Lul - la - by, sweet Je - sus, sleep now, Your cries hush.
Lu - laj - że, Je - zu - niu, me pie - ści - deł - ko,

Lul - la - by, sweet Je - sus, lul - la - by Ba - by, Sleep In - fant
Lu - laj - że, Je - zu - niu, lu - la - że, lu - laj, A Ty Go

1.
be - lov - ed, Moth - er will lull Thee.
Ma - tu - chno w płaczu u - tu - laj.

2.
Moth - er will lull Thee.
w płaczu u - tu - laj.

2. Close now Your wee eyelids, blinking
      with soft tears,
    Still Your wee lips trembling, for slumber
      time nears.
    Lullaby, sweet Jesus, lullaby, baby,
    Sleep Infant beloved, Mother will lull Thee.

2. *Zamknijże znużone płaczem powieczki,*
    Utulże zemdlone lkaniem usteczki. Lulajze . . .
    Lulajże piekniuchny nasz Aniołeczku,
    Lulajże wdzieczniuchny świata Kwiateczku Lulajże . . .
    Lulajże Różyczko najozdobniejsza,
    Lulajże Lilijko najprzyjemniejsza. Lulajże . . .

Hey Brothers, Are You Sleeping

Hej! Bracia! Czy Wy Spicie

English version–Josepha Contoski
Arr. –J. Krogulski
Adapted by Rose Polski Anderson

Allegretto

BARTOSZ:

1. Hey, broth-ers,
Hej! bra- cia

are you sleeping? Shep-herds, are you watching? E-vents nev-er heard of Now
czy wy spi- cie, czy wszyscy ba- czy- cie, dzi- wy nie-sły- cha- ne.

seem to be oc -cur-ring. O God! Dear God! What is this mys-te-ri-ous
dzi- wy nie-sły cha-ne. Oj trwo- ga dla Bo-ga co się

happ'ning? Bright the night! It is not day!__ Bright the night! It is not day!___
dzie- je, Jas- no w noc-y Choć nie dnieje, jas- no w noc-y choć nie dnie-je.

SHEPHERDS:

2. We shepherds are watch-ing, To us it is fright⌐ning, see-ing
I my też pa-trzy-my. a- le się bo- i- my, Pa- trząc

this great miracle. O God! Dear God! O, what is
na te dziw- y. Trwo- ga, Trwo- ga, dla Bo- ga

real – ly happ⌐ning? Hearts beat with great cor - ster
co się dzie- je. Od stra- chu ser – ce tru

na - tion, Hearts beat with our great con - ster - na - tion.
chle- je ser- ce tru- chle- je, truch- le- je.

Come, Shepherds, to the Stable

Do Szopy, Hej Pasterze

English version–Lucille Jasinski
Music Arr.–Rose Polski Anderson

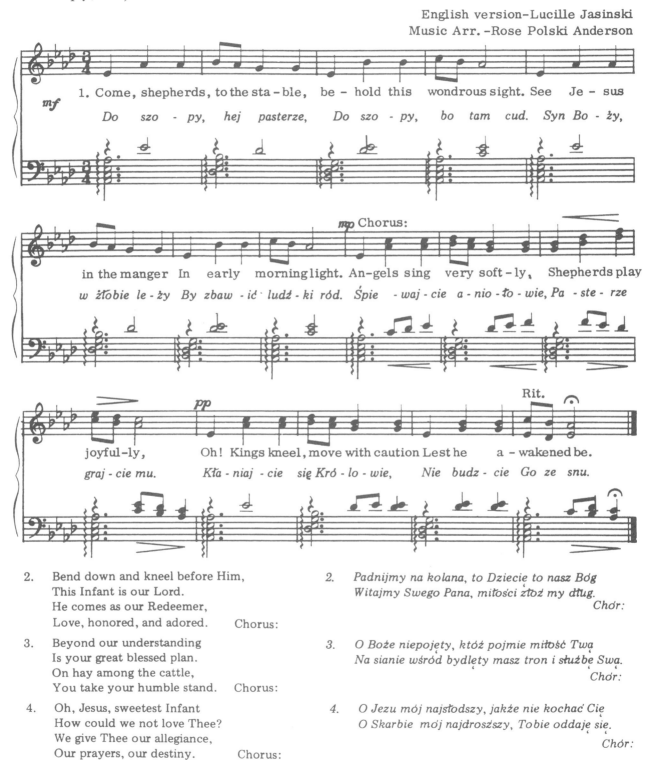

1. Come, shepherds, to the sta-ble, be-hold this wondrous sight. See Je-sus in the manger In early morning light. An-gels sing very soft-ly, Shepherds play joyful-ly, Oh! Kings kneel, move with caution Lest he a-wakened be.

Do szo-py, hej pasterze, Do szo-py, bo tam cud. Syn Bo-ży, w żłobie le-ży By zbaw-ić ludź-ki ród. Śpie-waj-cie a-nio-ło-wie, Pa-ste-rze graj-cie mu. Kła-niaj-cie się Kró-lo-wie, Nie budz-cie Go ze snu.

2. Bend down and kneel before Him,
This Infant is our Lord.
He comes as our Redeemer,
Love, honored, and adored. Chorus:

3. Beyond our understanding
Is your great blessed plan.
On hay among the cattle,
You take your humble stand. Chorus:

4. Oh, Jesus, sweetest Infant
How could we not love Thee?
We give Thee our allegiance,
Our prayers, our destiny. Chorus:

2. Padnijmy na kolana, to Dziecie to nasz Bóg
Witajmy Swego Pana, miłości złoż my dług.
Chór:

3. O Boże niepojęty, któż pojmie miłość Twą
Na sianie wśród bydlęty masz tron i służbę Swą.
Chór:

4. O Jezu mój najsłodszy, jakże nie kochać Cię
O Skarbie mój najdroszszy, Tobie oddaję sie.
Chór:

Polish Recipes

Mushroom Uszka*

Dough:
1 egg
½ c. water
2 tbsp. mashed potatoes
¼ t. salt
2 c. all-purpose flour

Filling:
1 c. chopped fresh mushrooms
1 small onion, chopped
2 tbsp. butter
2 tbsp. breadcrumbs
salt and pepper to taste

Place flour and salt in medium mixing bowl. Make a well in the center. Mix egg, water, and mashed potatoes. Pour into well. Mix until dough forms a ball. Place dough on floured board and knead until smooth and elastic, about 5 minutes. Cover with a bowl and let rest 10 minutes.

For filling, sauté mushrooms and onion in butter in skillet until tender. Stir in breadcrumbs, salt, and pepper. Cool mixture before using as filling.

Roll out half of the dough at a time until very thin. Cut into 2-inch squares. Place about ½ t. filling in the center of each

square of dough. Moisten edges with water. Fold square in half to form a triangle, pressing edges securely together. Lift up the two points of the base and pinch them together. As the dumplings are shaped, cover with a dampened towel and set aside. Cook dumplings in a pot of boiling salted water a large handful at a time for about 5 minutes or until tender. Dumplings may be cooked ahead, kept covered and refrigerated up to 3 days.

Makes 5 to 6 dozen dumplings

*To be added to Christmas Eve Beet Soup on recipe card.

Sauerkraut Filling (for *Pierogi*)*

1 tbsp. butter
1 tbsp. chopped onion
1 tbsp. flour
1 pint (1 lb.) sauerkraut, rinsed and drained
½ c. water
salt and pepper

Sauté onion in butter in medium saucepan until tender. Add flour and mix well. Stir in sauerkraut and water. Simmer, covered, about 1 hour. Season to taste with salt and pepper. Cool before using as filling for Pierogi.

Makes 2 cups

*See recipe card for Pierogi.

Polish Sausage with Sauerkraut (*Kielbasa Z Kapusta*)

1 lb. smoked Polish sausage
1 32-oz. jar sauerkraut, drained
salt and pepper
1 t. caraway seeds
2 slices bacon, diced
1 t. finely chopped onion
2 tbsp. flour

Place Polish sausage in a shallow pan; add a small amount of water and cook in a 350° oven for about 1 hour. If water still remains, place pan on top of range and sauté until sausage is lightly browned and water evaporates. Rinse sauerkraut with water; drain well.

Place sauerkraut in a pan and cover with water; add salt,

pepper, and caraway seeds. Simmer about 30 minutes. Sauté together bacon and onion in a skillet, until bacon is almost crisp and onion is soft. Stir in flour. If necessary, drain some of the water from sauerkraut; stir in bacon mixture. Cut browned sausage into 1-inch pieces; combine with sauerkraut.

Makes 4 to 6 servings

Northern Pike Polish Style *(Szczupak po Polsku)*

1 dressed northern pike, perch, or
    other white fish (2 lbs.)
1 carrot
1 onion
1 stalk celery
10 peppercorns
1½ t. salt
water
8 to 10 small boiled potatoes (optional)

Topping

¼ c. butter
6 hard-cooked eggs, finely chopped
¼ c. lemon juice
1 tbsp. chopped fresh dill or parsley
¾ t. salt
¼ t. pepper

Put fish into a large kettle. Add carrot, onion, celery, peppercorns, and salt. Add enough water to cover. Cover; boil gently about 15-20 minutes, or until fish flakes easily.

For topping, heat butter in a skillet. Add chopped eggs, lemon juice, dill or parsley, salt, and pepper. Cook 5 minutes, stirring frequently.

When fish is cooked, set it on a warm platter. Spoon topping over fish. Serve with boiled potatoes, if desired.

Makes 4 to 6 servings

The Culinary Arts Institute Polish Cookbook,
© 1976 Delair Publishing Company.

Hunter's Stew *(Bigos)*

3 lbs. diced cooked meat (use at
    least 3 of the following: beef,
    ham, lamb, sausage, veal, pork,
    venison or poultry)*
¼ lb. salt pork, diced
1 small onion, minced
1 leek, minced
1 tbsp. flour
½ lb. fresh mushrooms, sliced or 2
    cans (4 oz. each) sliced
    mushrooms (undrained)
½ to 1 c. water or bouillon
3 lbs. sauerkraut
1 t. salt
½ t. pepper
½ t. sugar
½ c. Madeira wine
chopped apples (optional)
heavy cream (optional)
cooked small potatoes (optional)

Fry salt pork until golden but not crisp in an 8-quart kettle. Add the onion and the leek. Sauté 3 minutes. Stir in flour. Add mushrooms with liquid and water or bouillon to kettle; simmer 5 minutes. Drain and rinse sauerkraut. Add to kettle along with cooked meat, salt, pepper, and sugar. Cover; cook over medium-low heat 1½ hours. Stir in wine. Add any of the remaining ingredients, if desired. Add more salt, pepper, and sugar to taste. Simmer 15 minutes; do not boil.

*If meat must be prepared especially for this stew, each piece should be braised separately. Put meat, poultry, or game into a Dutch oven with 1 carrot, 1 stalk celery, 1 onion, 1 parsnip, 1 clove garlic or 1 sprig parsley, 5 peppercorns, 1 cup water, and 1 cup wine. Simmer, covered, until meat is tender.

Makes 8 to 10 servings

The Culinary Arts Institute Polish Cookbook,
© 1976 Delair Publishing Company.

Kolacky

1 c. butter
1 8-oz.pkg. cream cheese
¼ t. vanilla extract
½ t. salt
2¼ c. all-purpose flour
thick jam or canned fruit filling,
    such as apricot or prune
confectioners' sugar

Cream butter and cream cheese until fluffy. Add vanilla. Add salt and flour to butter mixture, blending well. Cover and refrigerate dough several hours.

Roll out dough on lightly floured surface to ⅜-inch thickness. Cut out 2-inch circles or larger. Place on ungreased baking sheets. Make a thumbprint about ¼-inch deep

in each cookie and fill with jam. Bake at 350° until light brown, 12 to 15 minutes. Dust with confectioners' sugar.

Makes about 3½ dozen

Bow Ties (*Chrusciki*)

4 egg yolks
1 t. rum
¼ t. salt
2 c. unsifted all-purpose flour
½ pint dairy sour cream
hot oil for deep frying
confectioners' sugar

Beat egg yolks until lemon colored; blend in rum and salt. Add flour alternately with sour cream and mix until dough can be handled. Flour hands well and turn dough out onto a heavily floured board or pastry cloth; knead until smooth. Dough will be soft and sticky. Divide dough in half. Cover half of dough to prevent drying. Roll out the other half on floured board very thin

and cut into strips about 1½ inches × 5 inches. With a sharp knife, make a slit in the center of each square, then pull one of the corners through the slit. Heat oil to 350°. Add a few pastries at a time and fry until golden brown. Remove with slotted spoon and drain on absorbent paper. Dust with confectioners' sugar.

Makes about 4 dozen

Honey Cookies (*Pierniki*)

½ c. honey
½ c. sugar
2 eggs
½ t. vanilla extract
3 c. all-purpose flour
1 t. baking soda
½ t. salt
½ t. cinnamon
½ t. ginger
½ t. nutmeg
¼ t. cloves
1 egg white, beaten
48 blanched almond halves

Combine honey and sugar in a bowl; mix well. Beat in eggs and vanilla extract. In a separate bowl, blend flour, baking soda, salt, and spices. Stir into honey mixture. Knead to mix thoroughly; dough will be stiff. Shape dough into a ball. Wrap in plastic wrap. Let stand 2 hours.

Roll dough on a floured surface to ¼-inch thickness. Cut into

2½-inch rounds or other shapes. Brush top of each cookie with egg white. Press an almond onto center. Place on greased cookie sheets. Bake at 375° for 8 to 10 minutes. Cool on racks. Store in plastic bags for 8 to 10 days to mellow.

Makes about 4 dozen cookies

The Culinary Arts Institute Polish Cookbook,
© 1976 Delair Publishing Company.

Twelve-Fruit Compote

3 c. water
1 lb. mixed dried fruits including
    pears, figs, apricots, and peaches
1 c. pitted prunes
½ c. raisins or currants
1 c. pitted sweet cherries
2 apples, peeled and sliced or 6 oz.
    dried apple slices
½ c. cranberries
1 c. sugar
1 lemon, sliced
6 whole cloves
2 cinnamon sticks (3 in. each)
1 orange
½ c. grapes, pomegranate seeds, or
    pitted plums
½ c. fruit-flavored brandy

Combine water, mixed dried fruits, prunes, and raisins or currants in a 6-quart kettle. Bring to a boil. Cover; simmer about 20 minutes, or until fruits are plump and tender. Add cherries, apples, and cranberries. Stir in sugar, lemon, and spices. Cover; simmer 5 minutes. Grate peel of orange; reserve. Peel and section orange, removing all skin and white membrane. Add to fruits in kettle. Stir in grapes, pomegranate seeds,

or plums and brandy. Bring just to boiling. Remove from heat. Stir in orange peel. Cover; let stand 15 minutes.

Makes about 12 servings

The Culinary Arts Institute Polish Cookbook,
© 1976 Delair Publishing Company.

Acknowledgments

Cover CAF Press
2: © Grezegorz Roginski, Interpress
6: © Elliot Erwitt, Magnum
8: © Momatiuk/Eastcott from Woodfin Camp, Inc.
9: © Momatiuk/Eastcott from Woodfin Camp, Inc.
11: © J. Pokorski, Interpress
12: © Momatiuk/Eastcott from Woodfin Camp, Inc.
13: (Top) CAF Press
(Bottom) © Wojciech Krynsici, Interpress
15: © Wojciech Krynsici, Interpress
16: CAF Press
17: (Top) CAF Press
(Bottom) CAF Press
18: © Chuck Fishman, Contact
20: CAF Press
21: Art by Lydia Halverson
22: (Top) © Z. Wdowinski, Interpress
(Bottom) CAF Press
24: © Momatiuk/Eastcott from Woodfin Camp, Inc.
25: CAF Press
26: CAF Press
27: © J. Ochonski, Interpress
28: CAF Press
29: © Wojciech Krynsici, Interpress
30: © Chuck Fishman, Contact

32: CAF Press
33: © Chuck Fishman, Contact
35: CAF Press
38: CAF Press
39: CAF Press
40: © David Burnett, Contact
41: (Top) © Cezary Stominski, Interpress
(Bottom) CAF Press
42: J. Moak, Interpress
43: © Chuck Fishman, Contact
44: © Chuck Fishman, Contact
45: © Chuck Fishman, Contact
46: CAF Press
48: © Momatiuk/Eastcott from Woodfin Camp, Inc.
50: © Bruno Barbey, Magnum
53: CAF Press
55: CAF Press
57: Art by Lydia Halverson; CAF Press
58: CAF Press
60: © T. Prazmowski, Interpress
61: © S. Momot, Interpress
62: CAF Press
63: © Chris Niedenthal, Black Star
64: CAF Press